Immanuel Velikovsky
–
The Truth Behind The Torment

Ruth Velikovsky Sharon, Ph.D.

Paradigma

New, revised edition (2010).

Original edition (2003) by Xlibris Corporation

Published by   Paradigma Ltd.
                Internet: www.paradigma-publishing.com
                e-mail: info@paradigma-publishing.com

ISBN   978-1-906833-21-3 (Softcover edition)
       978-1-906833-61-9 (Hardcover edition)

Contents

Dedication
to my children

Carmel   Rafael   Naomi

and grandchildren
Elizabeth, Ashley, Cimarron,
Colby, Dylan, Canaan

Sculptures by Elisheva Velikovsky

Immanuel Velikovsky
Sculpture by Elisheva Velikovsky

"I was compelled by logic and by evidence to penetrate into so many premises of the house of science. I freely admit to having repeatedly caused fires, though the candle in my hand was carried only for illumination."

Immanuel Velikovsky

"When a true genius appears in the world, you may know him by this sign: that the dunces are all in confederacy against him."

Jonathan Swift's
Thoughts on Various Subjects

"All new and truly important ideas must pass through three stages: first, dismissed as nonsense, then rejected as against religion and, finally, acknowledged as true, with the proviso from initial opponents that they knew it all along."

Karl Ernst von Baer

"Many discoveries are reserved for the ages still to be, when our memory shall have perished. The world is a poor affair if it does not contain matter for investigation for the whole world in every age."

Immanuel Velikovsky

"Nature does not reveal all her secrets at once. We imagine we are initiated in her mysteries; we are, as yet, but hanging around her outer courts."

Immanuel Velikovsky

"What I am afraid of is not to be disputed, but to be dismissed without being read."

Immanuel Velikovsky

READERS DIGEST
Pleasantville, NY 10570

April 22, 1986

Ruth Velikovsky Sharon, Ph.D.
50 Deer Path
Princeton, NJ 08540

Dear Dr. Sharon:

It was a pleasure talking with you last week. I wanted you to know how moved I was by ABA*. I know from personal experience the cost that comes from the effort of writing such a memoir. You should be proud to leave such an honest and loving testament. Surely future generations, not only of your family, but of those who are captured by your father's life work, will be indebted to you.

Cordially,

(Signed) Fulton Oursler

---

* *Aba – The Glory and the Torment*, by Ruth Velikovsky Sharon, Ph.D., a biography of Immanuel Velikovsky, written by his daughter.

In 2004 Michael Lemonick taught a class at Princeton University:

FRS 124: Michael Lemonick, Princeton University

Science is constantly confronted with radical new ideas. Some will turn out to offer deep insights into the working of the universe. Others will be incorrect.

Science isn't always so good at distinguishing brilliant new ideas from the rest. As outsiders clamoring for attention and credibility often insist "they laughed at Einstein." In fact, they didn't, but they did laugh at Stanley Prusiner, who discovered the new infectious agent called the prion; at Alfred Wegener, who proposed continental drift; and of course at Galileo (though perhaps "laugh" isn't quite the right word for the behavior of the Inquisition).

In this course we'll look at the history of radical scientific ideas, and at the scientific community's response to them. We'll apply the lessons of that history to a number of recent or current scientific controversies, in which proponents of unconventional scientific theories have been battling for recognition by their mainstream colleagues. Finally, we'll have visits from working scientists who will help us understand how they deal with challenges to conventional wisdom – or to the conventional wisdom's distrust.

Dr. Ruth Velikovsky Sharon spoke to Michael Lemonick's class at Princeton University on Mon. March 1, 2004. She presented information about the controversy surrounding the publication of the book *Worlds in Collision* by her late father, Dr. Immanuel Velikovsky. Dr. Sharon described the scientific community's reaction to the book, and their successful attempts to stop Macmillan from publishing the book. She read quotes from numerous letters from scientists who condemned the book, while at the same time, bragging that they had never read the book. However, some of the letters included margin comments by Einstein, indicative that Einstein disagreed with Velikovsky's critics.

In addition to Dr. Sharon, Dr. C. J. Ransom, who has a Ph.D in Plasma Physics, spoke to the class about a number of 1950 predictions by Velikovsky and the subsequent verification of those predictions.

"HE IS A DANGEROUS CRANK"

1. " ... the promulgation of such *lies* – yes, *lies* ..."

2. "He seems to be one of our most erudite charlatans."

3. "He sought my endorsement of his theory. I was astonished. I looked around to see if he had a keeper with him."

4. "You know, of course, that I personally am a sympathetic friend of the thwarted and demented."

5. "Oh, no! No! Oh, no! Don't get trapped! He is a dangerous crank."

6. "He has misguided people like you in great numbers, and my advice is to shut the book and never look at it again in your lifetime."

Would you believe that these libelous statements were actually written by a former head astronomer at Harvard and other leading scientists to discredit and destroy a rival? What would drive a scientist to assassinate the character of another scientist? Why would other astronomers and physicists from universities throughout the country join an organized boycott to suppress the publication of a book and silence its author forever? Why was Albert Einstein one of the few scientists who was receptive to a revolutionary theory of the cosmos?

Over fifty years ago, interdisciplinary scholar Immanuel Velikovsky started one of the most significant scientific revolutions of the 20th century. The scientific establishment did not respond with dispassionate inquiry and civilized debate, but with violent opposition, a virtual holy war. This was followed by a conspiracy of silence and finally by widespread plagiarizing of his theories, which continues today. Vine Deloria, professor and Native American scholar, has called the suppression of Velikovsky's work "history's most close-minded libelous attack against a thinker daring to ask separate academic fields to achieve a unity of knowledge."

Velikovsky's experience is the quintessential story of the unappreciated genius, the heretic, who is such a threat to the status-quo that those in power organize in herd-like fashion to destroy not just a reputation, but a person's character and even his life. Faced with a message that so profoundly conflicted with their deeply held beliefs, mainstream science reacted by trying to kill the messenger.

Velikovsky's experience was not unlike those of other mavericks who challenged the prevailing ideology. Galileo was condemned to lifetime imprisonment by the church for basing his works on heretical Copernican theory. Mainstream inventor Thomas Edison proclaimed Nicola Tesla's discovery of alternating current as "a waste of time" that "nobody will use it, ever." Tesla was never credited for his genius until long after his death and, as with Velikovsky, Tesla's revolutionary ideas and patents were for years stolen by mainstream scientists.

Velikovsky never attacked his enemies, no matter what tactics they resorted to to undermine his works and character. Expecting some criticism and resistance, Velikovsky was not even remotely prepared for the onslaught of the scientific community. Thinking that it would take ten years for his theories to be accepted, he did not expect to be trampled without let-up until his death nearly 30 years after the publication of *Worlds in Collision*.

The relentless attacks took a toll on Velikovsky, but only his close friends and family knew it. The attacks wore down this brilliant, creative, energetic, optimistic mind and hurled him into a downward spiral of recurrent depression, suicide attempts and hospitalizations.

Velikovsky corrected many men and women in many fields of science – a crime compounded by his ability to write well along with pursuing the opportunity to present his theories to the general public.

No person wants to be told that much of his work and research during his lifetime is wrong. Giving credence to Velikovsky, one man, would have meant destroying the credence of volumes and volumes. By eliminating Velikovsky, subjecting him to ridicule, the scientific establishment in physics, astronomy, geology, history, etc., remained "intact".

Only an interdisciplinary scholar like Velikovsky would discover what was there all along. A great synthesizer who had an unusual capacity for grasping very disparate fields. However, academia considered it improper to cross boundaries. There was nothing about Velikovsky's mind that was improper. His mind was infinitely open and creative, able to cross hedges and make "fun" of all science for its nonsensical errors and its holier-than-thou attitude.

Not since the 17th century with Galileo's imprisonment by the church for his defense of Copernican theory has there been such a systematic suppression of truth by brute force. The names and details have changed, but the basic elements of the Galileo myth are the same. Both the Galileo story and the Velikovsky story represent the same age-old struggle between authority and free thought, power and knowledge, ignorance and enlightenment, darkness and light.

The Galileo myth symbolized the liberation of science from the yoke of religious superstition and authority. But, Galileo's enemy was actually the political power, which was embodied in the church, and in Velikovsky's case the same power now held by the scientific establishment. Society now treats the scientist with the same reverence once given to the bishops and cardinals of the 17th century. Scientific dogma vs. Velikovsky is the same 17th century clash between unreason and reason. The church attacked Galileo for revealing the conflicts between the Bible and science. More than 300 years later, the scientific establishment attacked Velikovsky for trying to resolve those conflicts.

Both Galileo and Velikovsky, bold and progressive free thinkers, represent the struggle of the authority of the individual vis a vis the consensus of the "herd"." Extremely confident of their ideas, both tried to stake specific claims to authority that the consensus was not about to relinquish. Velikovsky publicly called himself a "heretic", thus asserting this authority. Galileo wrote that " ... the authority of thousands of opinions is not worth as much as one tiny spark of reason in an individual man." Although Galileo truly believed that this "spark" was accessible to anyone open to it, the ruling elite must have perceived this opinion as arrogant.

Galileo has been described by scholars as a colorful figure, having a sense of honor and bravado, stubborn and having an inability to compromise. Never hesitant to voice disagreement, he loved a good fight and saw himself as the "true" interpreter of nature. Jesuit astronomers at one time carried on a dialogue with Galileo, but were then accused by the Dominican scientists of dissenting from orthodoxy. Galileo responded by pushing the Jesuits harder in the other direction, which only forced them to protect themselves by attacking Galileo, thus becoming his worst enemies.

Years after the church ordered Galileo to abstain from defending or teaching Copernicanism, he stubbornly defied authority by writing another book based on Copernican theories. When he asked permission from the same authorities to publish the new book, he was confronted about the prior warning. Galileo staunchly denied any memory of such an injunction. It was this obstinate act of defiance that resulted in his living the rest of his life under house arrest.

Velikovsky was described by those who knew him best, as humble and of the highest integrity. Tall, elegant, and even regal in his appearance, Velikovsky was charismatic and self-confident. He had superior oratory and persuasion skills, but never resorted to insults or dirty tactics to defend his point of view. He was described by social scientist, Alfred de Grazia, as always being "above the battle". "This is an achievement of a great leader – to be above the battle and yet direct it, not to lose one's dignity in a thicket of passionate verbiage, to be excommunicated and martyred without descending to the level of his opponents."

Like Galileo, Velikovsky considered himself an authority and asserted his views with a confidence that angered the scientific community. Albert Einstein told Velikovsky, with whom he developed a friendship during the last four years of Einstein's life, that it was adventurousness that made his adversaries all the more determined to stop him. Einstein said that Velikovsky should have presented his ideas as only tentative, not as bold assertions.

Velikovsky described himself as obstinate. His obstinacy, a trait that helped him persevere with the rigorous research necessary to formulate a revolutionary theory of the cosmos, was also a source of his suffering. Einstein told Velikovsky that he acted as if he were "the advocate retained by two natural forces: electricity and magnetism ... unyielding, never retreating."

What were the driving forces behind Velikovsky's unyielding tenacity? When asked how he could persevere for so many years to relentless opposition by the scientific establishment, Velikovsky answered, "It is the obstinacy of my race, the race of Marx, of Freud and of Einstein."

Being Jewish in Russia at the turn of the century was an immense challenge for Velikovsky's family because the government allowed Jews to comprise only 3% of the student body in Moscow's best schools. Early in life, Velikovsky learned perseverance from his mother, an ambitious woman and self-taught linguist, who succeeded in getting her three sons the best education in Russia. Private tutors in languages and other subjects and rigorous preparation for entrance exams consumed Velikovsky's childhood. Developing a persistent manner was essential for any Jew who wanted to be among the most highly educated in Moscow in the early 1900s.

"Giving up" was never an option for Velikovsky who had a deeply ingrained drive to excel and a passionately held belief that he was predestined for a "higher purpose" (from his father). Instead of choosing the path of Copernicus, who avoided persecution by waiting until his deathbed to publish his heretical theories, Velikovsky followed Galileo's course, persisting despite intense persecution.

Velikovsky, like Galileo, was a self-described lone heretic amidst a throng of persecutors. Galileo wrote, "Even the most trivial error is charged to me as a capital fault by the enemies of innovation, making it seem better to remain with the herd in error than to stand alone in reasoning correctly." Similarly, Velikovsky stated, "I was compelled by logic and by evidence to penetrate into so many premises of the house of science. I freely admit to having repeatedly caused fires, though the candle in my hand was carried only for illumination."

Albert Einstein and Velikovsky corresponded and spent many evenings together in Einstein's home, debating Velikovsky's theories. Einstein read *Worlds in Collision* three times and although he did not agree with all of Velikovsky's theories, he once told him, "Velikovsky, I think it is a great error that the scientists do not read your book – there is much that is important in it." Over time, Einstein came to agree with more of Velikovsky's views. But, partial validation from one of the world's finest minds did not satisfy Velikovsky.

Velikovsky's wish for "more" finally materialized when radio telescopes confirmed his hypothesis that radio noises were emitted by Jupiter.

This was a topic about which Velikovsky had relentlessly argued with Einstein for years.

Velikovsky wrote: "When I brought Einstein the news he was obviously much taken by what he learned. He was also embarrassed, for not only had he disregarded my request for this test, but also at our previous meeting he had stressed the great importance for the acceptance of a theory that it be able to generate correct predictions.

He stood up and asked, 'Which experiment would you like to have performed now?' I asked him to help me obtain radiocarbon tests to check on my reconstruction of ancient history. He was very emphatic in his desire to help me in this. This was our last meeting; he died a few days later." In fulfillment of his wish, his secretary wrote a letter to the Metropolitan Museum of Art with the request that some of the relics of Egypt be submitted for radiocarbon analysis.

Apart from Einstein and a handful of other scholars, the scientific community remained closed-minded. Among Velikovsky's harshest critics was Harlow Shapley. During the 1950's, Harlow Shapley, astronomer and head of the Harvard College Observatory, led the organized boycott of Macmillan's textbook division which forced Macmillan to suspend the publication of *Worlds in Collision*, which had reached the top of the national best-seller lists.

This was not the first time Shapley tried to suppress a scientific discovery that conflicted with his own theories. When Shapley was at the Mount Wilson Observatory (home of the Hubble telescope), Milton Humason, assistant to Edwin Hubble, presented him with a set of telescope plates showing evidence of Cepheid variables from beyond the Milky Way. Shapley, who was certain of himself, was having none of this. He launched into a shortened version of the same arguments he employed during the Great Debate, then calmly took out his handkerchief, turned the plates over, and wiped them clean of Humason's marks.

Helen Dukas
112 Mercer Street
Princeton N.J.

May 25, 1958

Dr. William Christopher Hayes
Department of Egyptology
Metropolitan Museum of Art
New York City

Dear Dr. Hayes,

I am writing to you at the request of Dr. Immanuel Velikovsky and because, as the secretary to the late Professor Einstein, I feel that I should inform you of the following matter.

During the course of the last eighteen months Professor Einstein had several discussions with Dr. Velikovsky – with whom he had friendly personal relations – about the latter's work. The last such discussion took place on April 8th. In the course of this conversation Professor Einstein said that he would write to you and suggest that you should give Dr. Velikovsky an opportunity to have his theory subjected to a radiocarbon test.

As I was present at this discussion I can assure you that Professor Einstein did intend to write that suggestion to you and but for the lateness of the hour the letter to you would have been written then and there.

Yours sincerely,

(Signed) Helen Dukas
Secretary to Albert Einstein

While conducting library research for his book on Freud and his heroes, Velikovsky became intrigued with articles about the geological formations around the Dead Sea. A friend pointed out to him that, according to the book of Genesis, the Dead Sea was a plain in the days of Abraham. Only when Moses and Joshua arrived there after the Israelites fled Egypt was a body of water found to exist. This raised questions in Velikovsky's mind: Was the Dead Sea formed in the days of the Exodus, the result of a natural catastrophe? Was this catastrophe also experienced in Egypt? When he read the texts of an ancient Egyptian papyrus, he found that the answer was yes. In fact, the descriptions of a catastrophe in the papyrus looked just like a copy of Exodus. The same held true when he examined the ancient texts of the Chinese, the Maya, the Hindus, the Babylonians and others.

For the next three years he went to numerous New York City public and university libraries, painstakingly gathering evidence that all pointed to the same conclusion that a global catastrophe took place in recent historical times, and that it was triggered by cosmic collisions in space. These findings, he knew, would have serious implications for the fields of astronomy, geology, physics and anthropology. This discovery marked the beginning of Velikovsky's reconstruction of ancient history and his interdisciplinary theory of the Earth and the cosmos.

From 1943 – 1950, Velikovsky shared his findings with scholars and scientists in different disciplines. Some scholars were open to Velikovsky's theories and of great help to him, such as egyptologist, Dr. Walter Federn, son of a well-known psychoanalyst and family friend, Dr. Paul Federn. Another, Professor Robert Pfeiffer of Harvard University, was critical, yet supportive, and encouraged Velikovsky to publish his findings. Horace Kallen, Dean of the Graduate Faculty of the New School for Social Research, who read Velikovsky's manuscripts, encouraged their publication.

In April 1946, Velikovsky attended a talk given by Harlow Shapley of the Harvard College Observatory. To test his theory of cosmic collisions and global catastrophe, he needed an analysis of the atmospheres of Venus and Mars. Shapley, it occurred to him, could complete these tests. He approached Shapley, asked him to read the manuscript and to consider doing two spectroscopic analyses.

Velikovsky to Shapley

> April 15, 1946
>
> Professor Harlow Shapley:
>
> In accordance with our conversation of April 13th, when you kindly agreed to test some of the conclusions of my historical cosmology (1940-41), I offer the following implications of my theory for testing: The atmosphere of the planet Mars consists mainly of argon and neon.
>
> (Signed) Im. Velikovsky

Velikovsky to Shapley

> April 17, 1946
>
> Dear Professor Shapley:
>
> May I offer another test which bears directly upon my reconstruction of historical cosmology:
> It is my conclusion that the planet Venus abounds in naphtha and its gases; therefore bands of gaseous hydrocarbons should be found in absorption spectrum of Venus.
>
> (Signed) Immanuel Velikovsky

Shapley agreed to this provided that Horace Kallen, Shapley's friend, also read and recommended it. Kallen was already familiar with the book and encouraged its publication. Despite Kallen's recommendation in writing, Shapley refused to read the manuscript and conduct the analyses, saying Velikovsky's claims were sensational.

Shapley to Velikovsky

May 15, 1946

Dear Sir:

Dr. Shapley asks me to write you that your unelaborated statements or arguments about the atmospheres of the planets are not sufficient grounds for astronomers to examine your claims. He suggests that you talk the matter over with the astronomers at Columbia University.

Very truly yours,

(Signed) Secretary to Dr. Shapley

This was only the beginning of a life-long attack by the scientific establishment of Velikovsky's work, and Shapley would become the leader of the pack.

Kallen to Velikovsky

THE GRADUATE FACULTY OF POLITICAL AND SOCIAL SCIENCES NEW YORK, NY

May 21, 1946

Dear Velikovsky:

The vigor of the scientific imagination that you show, the boldness of your construction and the range of your inquiry and information fill me with admiration.

(Signed) H. M. Kallen

Velikovsky to Shapley

Written May 23, 1946
Sent 26

Professor Harlow Shapley
Harvard College Observatory
Cambridge, Mass.

Dear Professor Shapley:

I thank you for your letter of May 15th. There is nothing I would like better than to substantiate my statements of April 15th and 27th by arguments. In the first two files of my Ms, I show that in the second and first millennia before this era, changes occurred in the constitution of the solar system and in the position of Earth, Moon, Venus and Mars. Presented in these few words my conclusion may appear strange, but they are built upon an extensive material from diverse fields of science.

---

cont'd

Velikovsky to Shapley (cont'd)

I claim the presence of hydrocarbon bands in the spectrum of Venus; this may be regarded as a crucial test for an important part of my theory.

In a special work I deal with those implications of my historical cosmology which concern Newtonian gravitation.

I shall be very grateful for time and attention you may give my work.

(Signed) Velikovsky

Kallen to Shapley

THE GRADUATE FACULTY OF POLITICAL AND SOCIAL SCIENCES NEW YORK, NY

May 25, 1946

Dear Shapley:

Dr. Immanuel Velikovsky tells me that he has hinted to you his remarkable theories regarding changes in the structure of the solar system during historical times.

He tells me also that one crucial point of his theory involves the content of the atmosphere of Venus which, if his theory is valid, would show petroleum gases, and that he has suggested to you a spectroscopic analysis of the atmosphere of Venus for those gases.

I have just finished reading his manuscript. After taking it up, I could not put it down.

I am myself impressed by what Dr. Velikovsky has had to say. I feel as eager as he to have it undergo the crucial test which the spectroscopic analysis he suggests would be.

(Signed) H. M. Kallen, Dean

Shapley to Kallen

HARVARD COLLEGE OBSERVATORY
CAMBRIDGE, MASS

May 27, 1946

Dear Kallen:

The sensational claims of Dr. Immanuel Velikovsky fail to interest me as much as they should.

In other words, if Dr. Velikovsky is right, the rest of us are crazy.

And seriously, that may be the case. It is, however, improbable.

(Signed) Harlow Shapley

Dictated by Dr. Shapley:
Signed in his presence

Kallen to Shapley

THE GRADUATE FACULTY OF POLITICAL AND
SOCIAL SCIENCES NEW YORK, NY

May 31, 1946

Dear Shapley:

I myself am much impressed both with the data that Velikovsky has assembled and his method of handling them. The first effect is one of shock, and then you get intrigued.

(Signed) H. M. Kallen

Velikovsky to Kallen

June 16, 1946

Dear Professor Kallen:

Six days after Professor Shapley wrote to you on May 27th, there was an announcement by Dr. O. Struve which I copied for you from the N. Y. Times of June 3. He and his colleagues developed a new method of spectroscoping the atmospheres of the planets.

P.S. I would like to believe that the correspondence between you and Shapley will be kept safe for future recording.

Kallen to Fadiman

HORACE M. KALLEN
66 WEST TWELFTH STREET
NEW YORK, NEW YORK

October 31, 1947

Mr. Clifton Fadiman
104 East 37th Street
New York 16, New York

Dear Fadiman:

Even if I thought that Velikovsky's theories were entirely un-grounded I should treat them as an extraordinary achievement of the scientific and historical imagination and deal with them with the seriousness that any high and unusual philosophic speculation deserves. But it is my belief that Velikovsky has supported his theses with substantial evidence and has made an effective and persuasive argument.

In writing about him and his opinions it is not necessary to "go overboard". You need only call attention to the originality of the point of view, the novelty of the approach, and its implications if further inquiry by other people should substantiate the Velikovsky findings. These are extremely exciting on their merits and I am very glad that you will call them to public attention in '47 Magazine. Do please send me a copy or an offprint when your piece appears.

Cordially yours,
(Signed) H. M. Kallen

Velikovsky sent his manuscript to John O'Neill, science editor of the New York Herald Tribune. Soon thereafter, O'Neill wrote of Velikovsky's theory in an article that appeared in that paper on august 11, 1946. By May 1947, after several publishers turned down the publication of Velikovsky's book, Macmillan Company agreed to publish *Worlds in Collision*. A contract was signed, and Velikovsky began the task of completing the final draft. By February 1949, the galleys were ready and the book would be released in April of that year.

Before the publication of *Worlds in Collision*, Frederick L. Allen, Editor-in-chief of *Harper's* Magazine, was authorized by Macmillan to present an article summarizing Velikovsky's book. This was written by Eric Larrabee, an editor at *Harper's*, and was titled *The Day The Sun Stood Still*. It appeared in the January 1950 issue of the magazine and sold out in just a few days. It provoked many angry attacks and protest letters to *Harper's* from scientists around the country.

Only a few days after this article appeared, a Japanese astronomer observed the first cosmic collision in modern times, between Mars and a planetoid.

1879 Coventry Road
Columbus 12, Ohio

January 25, 1950

Editor, Harper's Magazine
New York NY

Dear Sir:

The article on the sun standing still is an obvious hoax of astronomical proportions. Why don't you hire an intelligent eighth grader to assist your Science Editor in sorting out trash?

With sympathy
Very sincerely yours,

(Signed) Alfred Lande,
Professor of Physics,
The Ohio State University

Murdock to Harper's

YALE UNIVERSITY
Department of Anthropology
New Haven, Connecticut

January 2, 1950

Dear Mr. Allen:

I am sorry to report that Harper's "has been had."

It is a shameful thing that Harper's should perpetrate such a hoax on its readers. My favorite magazine for thirty years has suddenly sunk to the level of a Hearst Sunday supplement. Unless you aspire to a ranking among the science fiction "pulps," you had better take strenuous steps to rehabilitate yourselves.

What sudden malaise can have led you to belch forth this monstrous hybrid of naiveté and sensation mongering?

Yours in acute disillusionment,

George P. Murdock
Professor of Anthropology

HARVARD UNIVERSITY
Department of Physics
Cambridge, Massachusetts

January 27, 1950

Editors, Harper's Magazine
49 East 33rd Street
New York, New York

Dear Sirs:

In the particular case of the article in question, it would be patently obvious to any well trained graduate student in physics that the original version of "The Day the Sun Stood Still" is the product of a "crackpot."

Very sincerely yours,

(Signed) Dr. Lewis M. Branscomb
Professor of Anthropology

February 28, 1950

Harper's

Dear Sirs:

I see by the response to "The Day The Sun Stood Still", that the Real and True Scientists who deal in reliable knowledge carry on in their harmless little sport of tearing apart their fellow-man and throwing him to the vultures.

E.B.
Royal Oak, Mich.

HARVARD COLLEGE OBSERVATORY
CAMBRIDGE 3, MASS

January 16, 1950

The Editors
Harper's Magazine
49 East 33rd Street
New York 16, N.Y.

Gentlemen:

I cannot understand how a supposedly reliable magazine could possibly have published "The Day the Sun Stood Still." Dr. Velikovsky's so-called evidence has no conceivable basis in scientific fact.

Publication of this article constitutes a serious disservice to the cause of science, history, and religion. By citing scriptural authority in a pseudo scientific fashion, the author may well reopen the old warfare between science and theology. This article is a black mark on Harper's record and an insult to the intelligence of its readers, who have a reasonable right to expect authority in the publication.

Cannot the editors distinguish fact from "crank" hypothesis? Do they not realize that misguided incompetents, the world over, pour out a continuous effusion of unscientific doctrines?

To make matters worse, you will undoubtedly receive letters of commendation from many individuals, who have been deluded by the mere fact that Harper's has published the material.

You will imply that Dr. Velikovsky will, in an early issue, debate the correctness of his dramatic imaginings. Shall we also anticipate that you will soon espouse the cause of black magic as opposed to modern medicine, alchemy as a substitute for atomic research? Perhaps you will introduce an ultra-modern scheme of arithmetic, based on the postulate $2 + 2 = 5$, as an aid to understanding Dr. Velikovsky's argument.

Very truly yours,

(Signed) Donald H. Menzel

Harper's to Menzel

HARVARD COLLEGE OBSERVATORY
CAMBRIDGE 3, MASS

February 27, 1950

The Editors
Harper's Magazine
49 East 33rd Street
New York 16, N.Y.

Dear Dr. Menzel:

Thank you for your letter about the Velikovsky theory and the article summarizing it which appeared in our January number. We had hoped to acknowledge letters such as yours sooner than this, but at the same time we wanted to wait until a representative sampling had come in, in order to place the reactions provoked by the article in better perspective. You are certainly not alone in expressing doubts about it.

May we assure you, however, that we printed "The Day the Sun Stood Still" in full awareness of the degree to which it was

cont'd

bound to conflict with accepted doctrines in many sciences. For this reason, we investigated Dr. Velikovsky's credentials and secured the opinions of those who had read his book. To date only one scientist who has read it (actually the science editor of a newspaper) has expressed an adverse opinion, and the point on which his skepticism hinges has been specifically questioned by a number of scientists who have read Dr. Velikovsky's discussion of gravitational theory, which will form a part of a later work. Undoubtedly there will be further criticism of the book; this criticism may lead to complete or partial rejection of Dr. Velikovsky's hypothesis; but under the circumstances we felt obliged, however disconcerting its conclusions might be, to treat seriously an impressive body of writing which, on our own observation, is copiously documented, internally coherent, and supported by material of an evidential character.

We can fully understand your deep concern at the appearance of an unorthodox approach to many specialized fields of investigation, but in all frankness we did not anticipate that it would be condemned quite as categorically before the book itself was published and the author had a hearing before the academic world. We trust that the objections which Dr. Larrabee's article raised in your own mind will not prevent you, when Worlds in Collision and its subsequent volumes are available, from deciding for yourself whether or not they warrant the impartial and dispassionate attitude which is customary in science, and which is its pride and most hopeful promise.

We have passed on your letter to the editor of our "Letters" column, on the chance that he may be able to use all or part of it in the March issue of the magazine.

HARVARD COLLEGE OBSERVATORY
CAMBRIDGE, MA

December 9, 1963

Mr. Eric Larrabee
12 East 9th Street
New York 3, New York

My dear Mr. Larrabee:

The validity of Velikovsky's claim to having predicted a high temperature for the surface depends upon whether or not his theory of the recent origin of Venus, as a comet born from Jupiter (or anywhere else for that matter) is correct. I do not know of a single scientist who believes Velikovsky correct. I think that there might be a low form of life in the upper atmosphere of Venus, despite the inhabitability of the surface.

In the scientific sense, Velikovsky offers no evidence whatever. He presents a curiously selected mixture of scientific oddities, a mish-mash of unsupported theory, and dislocated history.

Well, to come back to earth, I fear, Mr. Larrabee, that you and I are bound to continue on the opposite sides of the fence. As I recall your position long ago, you felt committed to the Velikovsky hypothesis. You did not want to crawl back. But if you are going to write on scientific subjects, I suggest that you at least learn how a scientist thinks.

Sincerely yours,

(Signed) Donald H. Menzel
Director

Menzel to Gustafson (21 years later)

HARVARD COLLEGE OBSERVATORY
CAMBRIDGE, MASS

April 21, 1971

Mr. Tom Gustafson Jr.
124 St. Paul's Place
South Bend, Indiana 46616

Dear Mr. Gustafson:

I did become, somewhat indirectly, an important figure in the controversy over Velikovsky. With respect to his theories of catastrophism, I know of no major scientist who supports his views. Those who have supported him are, for the most part, individuals who have essentially no scientific background and are unable to appreciate the scientific method. Whatever Velikovsky did, it was certainly not scientific method. My views on his work have not changed.

What made me even madder, however, was the audacity of that nincompoop of a writer, for Harper's, who had absolutely no scientific ability, to stick his neck out and proclaim the Velikovsky line.

But, Velikovsky was an absolute idiot. He was trying to piece together bits of uncertain history.

I thought that Larrabee might be a reasonable person. He kept saying he was going to stick to his guns and eventually he felt that he would prove that Velikovsky was right and that I was wrong.

Sincerely yours,

(Signed) Donald H. Menzel

One of the attacks was from Harlow Shapley, the astronomer from Harvard University, who refused to conduct the spectroscopic tests. He wrote two letters to James Putnam, Velikovsky's editor at Macmillan.

Shapley to Editorial Dept., Macmillan Co.

HARVARD COLLEGE OBSERVATORY
CAMBRIDGE, MASS

January 18, 1950

I have heard a rumor from a source that should be reliable that possibly the Macmillan Company will not proceed to the publication of Dr. Velikovsky's "Worlds In Collision". This rumor is the first item with regard to the Velikovsky business that makes for sanity. What books you publish are of course no affair of mine; and certainly I would depend on your expert judgment rather than on my own feelings in the matter. But I thought it might be well to record with you that the few scientists with whom I have talked about this matter (and this includes the President of Harvard University and all of the members of the Harvard Observatory staff) are not a little astonished that the great Macmillan Company famous for its scientific publications would venture into the Black Arts without rather careful refereeing of the manuscript.

The Velikovsky declaration of hypothesis or creed that the sun stood still is the most errant nonsense of my experience, and I have met my share of crackpots.

... to one reader of Macmillan's scientific books the aforementioned rumor is a great relief.

Sincerely yours,

(Signed) Harlow Shapley

Both Putnam and George Brett responded to Shapley's letters; Brett saying that opinions from three scholars would he sought before publication.

Putnam to Shapley

THE MACMILLAN COMPANY
NEW YORK, NY

January 24, 1950

Dear Professor Shapley:

Thank you very much for your letter of January 18 which has been referred to me, as I have been working with Dr. Velikovsky on his book, "Worlds In Collision," for several years. I am afraid that the rumor, which you have heard, is unfounded, as the book is about to go to press and we plan to publish it on March 28.

Obviously it is a most controversial theory, and we have long faced the fact that there will be a great diversity of reaction to the book. As to Dr. Velikovsky's scholarly attainments, you will perhaps be interested in the brief summary of biographical data regarding him, which I am enclosing.

I appreciate very much the spirit in which your letter was written, but I cannot believe that our publication of this book, which is presented by us as a theory, will affect your feeling toward our publications in the scientific field.

Sincerely yours,

(Signed) James Putnam

Shapley to Putnam at Macmillan

HARVARD COLLEGE OBSERVATORY
CAMBRIDGE, MASS

January 25, 1950

It will be interesting a year from now to hear from you as to whether or not the reputation of the Macmillan Company is damaged by the publication of "Worlds In Collision".

If I remember correctly, several years ago (perhaps only three or four) Dr. Velikovsky, with an introduction from Horace Kallen, or some other acquaintance of mine, met me in a New York hotel. He sought my endorsement of his theory. I was astonished. I looked around to see if he had a keeper with him. I tried, but rather futilely, to explain to him that if the earth could be stopped in such a short space of time it would overthrow all that Isaac Newton had done; it would have wrecked all life on the surface of the planet; it would have denied all the laborious and impartial findings of paleontology; it would have made impossible that he and I could meet together in a building in New York City less than four thousand years after this tremendous planetary event.

Dr. V. seemed very sad. But somehow I felt he was feeling sorry for me and the thousands of other American physical scientists and geologists and historians who have been so, so wrong. (You may be able to report that Dr. V. has never been in New York and that my consultant was another planet handler.)*

You cannot wonder that I looked for a keeper. But of course if he and Macmillan are right, I should rather be looking for the million keepers who should be in charge of the million of us who are not willing to change the facts and careful recordings of nature, and the laws of nature, in the interests of exegesis.**

Naturally you can see that I am interested in your experiment. And, frankly, unless you can assure me that you have done things like this frequently in the past without damage, the publication must cut me off from the Macmillan Company. But that is a triviality.***

cont'd

Shapley to Putnam at Macmillan (cont'd)

One of my colleagues by request is writing a commentary on Larrabee's article, and, being also a classicist, will probably have a good time. I don't suppose there would be any chance that you would send to me for this colleague an early copy of the proof sheets so that it will be Dr. V. who is discussed and not Mr. Larrabee?

Yes, it will be an interesting experiment. Incidentally, I suppose you have checked up on the references of Dr. V. He certainly has had a brilliant and varied career, and is remarkably versatile. It is quite possible that only this "Worlds In Collision" episode is intellectually fraudulent.

Sincerely yours,

(Signed) H. Shapley

Velikovsky had given Einstein letters and a summary of some of his ideas on which Einstein wrote comments in the margins.

* Einstein's comment: "Unbelievable arrogance."
** Einstein's comment: "Stupid remark."
*** Einstein's comment: "Mean!"

HARVARD COLLEGE OBSERVATORY
CAMBRIDGE, MASS

February 9, 1950

Dear Mr. Brett:

I note that you are seeking comment of additional referees. Therefore you and your colleagues may be interested in the enclosed first draft of an article written by request for a monthly magazine by one of my colleagues at the Harvard Observatory.

Since writing you I find that I have in my files a letter from the author, and also a pamphlet he sent me entitled "Cosmos without Gravitation." It was, of course, properly filed away with the "curiosa," where we put the writings of the Flat Earth Society, the products of the over-throwers of the theory of relativity, the flying saucer reports and the like. Such contributions, as you know, are nearly always published by the author. We try to look sympathetically at all such receipts at the Observatory, and acknowledge most of them. It would be unfortunate if through a hasty or prejudiced examination we should overlook a Ramanujan.

Sincerely yours,

(Signed) Harlow Shapley

Two out of three scientists recommended publishing "Worlds in Collision." Professor C. W. van der Merwe, Chairman of the Department of Physics at New York University, was one of the three who approved the book for publication.

When Shapley did not get the results he hoped for from Macmillan, he changed his strategy. He wrote a letter to Ted O. Thackrey, previously chief editor of the *New York Post* and then publisher of *The Compass*, a progressive newspaper. Thackrey had reprinted Eric Larrabee's *Harper's* article and wrote a favorable editorial about Velikovsky's work and its value to science.

Shapley to Thackrey

HARVARD COLLEGE OBSERVATORY
CAMBRIDGE, MASS

February 20, 1950

Mr. Ted Thackrey
The Compass

Dear Ted:

Somebody has done you dirt. They got you to republish Larrabee's article from the January Harper's Magazine. *Colliers also has given this crank a great run, and several other presumably reputable publications have handled the stuff with a flat pen.*

In my rather long experience in the field of science, this is the most successful fraud that has been perpetrated on leading American publications. To me the article seems so transparent that I am surprised that Harper's and Macmillan would handle it. I am not quite sure that Macmillan is going through with the publication, because that firm has perhaps the highest reputation in the world for the handling of scientific books.

A representative of Max Ascoli's magazine, The Reporter, called me up a few weeks ago and asked me to write a refutation of my comment. My colleague, Mrs. Cecilia Payne Gaposchkin, has written such a paper for The Reporter, and I suppose it will be forthcoming soon. I enclose a copy. It occurs to me that The Compass might like to republish (with permission) this comment from an American astronomer of the highest standing.

A few years ago this Dr. V. sent me a copy of his pamphlet entitled "Cosmos without Gravitation." I filed it away with the other crank literature that comes to a scientific laboratory. We could dig out several equally plausible writings, mostly published at the author's expense. We have the publications of the Flat Earth Society – desperately sincere. We have the theories of the origin of the solar system by the Fuller Brush man of Florida. We have the writings of the men who unfortunately were unable ever to go to school, but have herewith overthrown the theories of Einstein (as Dr. V. has overthrown Darwin and Newton and all the rest).

A number of astronomical groups have talked about this business, and their sad conclusion generally is that we are in an age of decadence where nonsense stands higher than experiment and learning.

Of course one should not pay any serious attention to these matters and I certainly would not have done so if The Compass had not reprinted, apparently with a straight face, the Larrabee article.

This man Dr. V. came to me in New York several years ago and asked me to endorse his work so that he could get it published. I pointed out to him that if he were right then all that Isaac Newton ever did was wrong. Nevertheless, we seem to have built up a civilization, and the hotel in which we were standing, on account of the contribution of Newton and others of his kind.

You know of course that I personally am a sympathetic friend of the thwarted and demented, and have no high respect for formalism, and none at all for orthodoxy. But this "Sun stood still" stuff is pure rubbish, of the level of the astrological hocus-pocus, except that Dr. V. has read widely as well as superficially and can parade a lot of technical terms which apparently he has not mastered. But if he had mastered them who would want to publish his stuff!

Sincerely yours,

(Signed) Harlow Shapley

THE DAILY COMPASS
NEW YORK, NY

February 27, 1950

Dr. Immanuel Velikovsky
526 West 113th Street
New York, New York

Dear Dr. Velikovsky:

I am forwarding herewith a copy of a letter to me under date of February 20th from Professor Harlow Shapley. I will send you a copy of my reply when I have had the opportunity to dictate it, which will be some time early next week.

Sincerely,

(Signed) T. O. Thackrey
Editor and Publisher

Shapley asked Thackrey to print a refutation of Velikovsky's work, an article written by his astronomer colleague, Cecilia Payne-Gaposchkin, a copy of which he attached to the letter. Cecilia Payne-Gaposchkin had not read *Worlds in Collision* which had not yet been published. It turns out that Shapley had also distributed this mimeographed article to many members of the scientific community around the country.

March 7, 1950

Dear Harlow:

I have delayed an answer to your letter of February 20 until I felt reasonably recovered from my initial reaction to its content.

I could not feel that our friendship was worth retaining if I were not as frank in my reply as you undoubtedly were being with me. In the first place, I feel that I must take with you as sharp an exception to your series of wholly unwarranted and unfounded characterizations of Dr. Velikovsky, as I have had occasion to take in another field when your political views have led to nearly as unwarranted an assault upon your own integrity.

I am genuinely shocked, in re-reading your letter, at the epithets you have seen fit to use in characterizing Dr. Velikovsky, a man of unusual integrity and scholarship, whose painstaking approach to scientific theory is at least a match for your own.

I find in your first paragraph a reference to "this crank" and an innuendo that publishers who will handle his stuff are only "presumably" reputable.

In your second paragraph, you characterize Dr. Velikovsky's suggestions not only as "fraud," but a "most successful fraud perpetrated" on publications. You further suggest that, evidently through your efforts, there is now some question about whether Macmillan will go through with the publication, thus not only confessing to do direct damage, but to provide, some evidence of having, successfully damaged Dr. Velikovsky's work.*

I go now on the final paragraph, in which you remark that you are personally "a sympathetic friend of the thwarted and demented." I must conclude you intend to further characterize Dr. Velikovsky, since it could have no other possible purpose for construction. Further, you declare that the "stuff" is "pure rubbish" on the level of the astrological hocus-pocus and then

cont'd

go on to characterize Dr. Velikovsky as one who has read widely "as well as superficially."

It so happens that my acquaintanceship with Dr. Velikovsky antedates the course of which I have ample opportunity to verify from a wide variety of unimpeachable sources Dr. Velikovsky's scholarship and high integrity as an individual. His claims as to his studies, his background and his degrees have consistently, and without exception, been on the modest side.

It seems to me that you are making both a personal and professional mistake – a gravely serious and dangerous one – by the totally unscientific and viciously emotional character of your attack upon Dr. Velikovsky and his work. **

I am writing this advisedly, since it is obvious that you have seen fit to unleash a series of attacks, by no means directed to me alone, both against Dr. Velikovsky and against his work, without ever once having taken the trouble to examine his work or even glance at the evidential research with which it has been accompanied.

I submit that, at the time of writing your letter, you had neither read the manuscript of Dr. Velikovsky's "Worlds In Collision," nor a single piece of evidence in its support. At the most, it is possible that you had examined superficially a popularization of a very small portion of this work by Eric Larrabee of Harper's Magazine.

It would be totally presumptuous of me to make the slightest effort to maintain the scientific validity of the conclusions which Dr. Velikovsky has stated as tentative theses, growing out of the historical evidence which he has amassed. But I think it is equally evident that you are at the present time, despite your scientific attainments, in an even less valid position to quarrel with Dr. Velikovsky's evidence or his conclusions, since you have not taken the trouble to examine either.

In fact, it is impossible for me not to be alarmed at the intensity and character of the attack, particularly from an individual of your scientific attainment, which is based so completely on hearsay and emotional reaction. I am sure you would yourself hesitate to reach a conclusion about the nature of a planet without having examined with care all of the available evidence. And yet, you have had no hesitancy in proclaiming a distinguished scholar an impostor, a charlatan and a fraud and characterizing his work as pure rubbish.

That your course of action is, on its face, both morally and criminally slanderous and libelous, would have been perfectly evident to me, even had I not made a most thorough study of the law in relationship to slander and libel, having spent some six years in acquiring a degree in the law with the primary purpose of backgrounding myself in the essentials of newspaper publishing.

Certainly, it is possible that the evidence adduced by Dr. Velikovsky is scientifically inconclusive, but to maintain that it is rubbish merely because of a possible (though by no means certain) conflict with another working hypothesis, without even having bothered to make an examination of the evidence is, it seems to me, clearly nonsense, even when the nonsense is uttered by one who has achieved such an eminently responsible position in the field of astronomy as yourself. ***

I beg of you, in all earnestness, to consider your course of conduct in this matter and contrast it with the high standards you set before your students, before proceeding further in your campaign to destroy a man whom you do not know and to damn a theory about which you obviously know nothing.

I did take the trouble to read the article which you had prepared by Mrs. Cecilia Payne-Gaposchkin. I have no presumption of scientific knowledge in her field and no basis for accepting or rejecting the scientific theories expounded in her article. I do, however, have a criticism of the main tenor of the article itself, which is as follows:

1. The article is an attack upon a book which the writer has not read.

cont'd

2. In at least two instances, the article sets up straw men and then proceeds to demolish the straw men. In other words, the article attributes to Dr. Velikovsky's statements which are not made either by him or in his manuscript, and then proceeds to quarrel with those statements as though they were authentic.

This is, to say the least, a most unscientific method of criticism.

Sincerely,
(Signed) Ted. O. Thackrey

****

---

* Einstein's comment (cf. p. 38): "Bravo!"
** Einstein's comment: "Ja!" ("Yes!")
*** Einstein's comment: "Gut!" ("Good!")
**** Einstein's comment (at the end of the letter): "The man is fine and smart. (Compliment)"

HARVARD COLLEGE OBSERVATORY
CAMBRIDGE, MASS

March 8, 1950
Confidential

Dear Ted:

I apologize immediately for having written such disparaging remarks about an acquaintance of yours. My astonishment stands, but so does my apology.

I now have your telegram, and I realize that I should cancel those parts of your letter which suggest that I made damning statements without any evidence to judge Dr. Velikovsky's theories or methods of thinking or evaluation of evidence. "Cosmos without Gravitation" is an unusual work in a real world.

The fact that you have known him well and apparently have discussed his contributions in a wide field of scholarship does convince me that I should restrain my comments and judgments to the astrophysical and celestial mechanical details of Dr. Velikovsky's conclusions. But I have studied history and classics also.

Last week's Science News Letter, incidentally, included statements on the Larrabee article from men in other fields – all of distinction, I believe – and they seem to be unfavorable. Time of this week also takes a dim view.

I myself am not writing anything in response to Dr. Velikovsky or Larrabee or anyone. In fact, the only hot communication I have made was this letter to you. I certainly wrote it to the wrong person!*

In half a dozen groups, chiefly of Harvard University professors (and they are not all ill-mannered, injudicious, or dumb), without exception I have found no one whose views about the Reader's Digest survey of the volume, to say nothing of Larrabee's article, were other than mine. Many, like Ickes in the New Republic, took the whole business as a joke. Wasn't Larrabee a Lampoon editor?

cont'd

Shapley to Thackrey (cont'd)

Perhaps I wrote you that a vice-president of the American Astronomical Society should send a protest to Macmillan, the famous publisher of highly reputable scientific books; but I said immediately, and so did many others, that such an action would merely give greater publicity to Dr. Velikovsky's contributions. Freedom to publish is a basic freedom.

I do not have my earlier letter before me, but I hope I wrote, and I think I did, that Dr. V., and all others with "unorthodox" theories which if true upset a very large section of the science on which we have built our industrial modern civilization – that all such authors certainly have a full right to publish their conclusions.

Our trouble about the Macmillan Company and Harper's, if you call it trouble, was that such publications seem to throw doubt on the care with which they referee other manuscripts on which we want to depend. There was no fear whatever of being misled by Dr. Velikovsky's views.

I remember just now that I have been circularized by some church organ that is trying to find what people think of the bearing of Dr. Velikovsky's work on the biblical miracles, and they asked me also, to reply; and my reply had to be the same brief, sincere, and strong statement that one cannot build a heavily mathematical and tested theory of the laws of motion around the myths and bibles of the past.

In conclusion, I remember that Dr. Velikovsky was a very nice personality, quiet, modest, and apparently genuinely sorry that I and the likes of me had been so misled by Isaac Newton, Laplace, Lagrange, Simon Newcomb, the great, national observatories in all the leading countries. He was, in fact, quite charming, as I remember him. No doubt, from what you say, he is a deep scholar in some fields? I have not yet seen statements from scholars to this effect, and possibly you would not value them highly if they should speak adversely. They squabble among themselves – these philosophers of the ancient times and of the fragmentary records. But it is hard to quarrel with a differential equation, or with numbers; and therefore the trained astronomers and physicists, almost to the last man, will insist on the fallacy of Dr. Velikovsky's celestial mechanics. Even the planetarium lecturer, who is almost totally unknown to astronomers, was evasive in his not unfavorable comments.

In signing off I again apologize for the vigor of my language; but, following the precedent of one Galileo, I stand fast on the evidence and the assertions that Venus did not participate in the stopping of the rotating of the earth some fifteen hundred years B.C. <u>One cannot be dishonest in such matters and remain a scientist.</u>**

But I insist on remaining your friend. Neither Dr. V. nor the planet-comet Venus should get between us.

Sincerely yours,

(Signed) Harlow

---

* Einstein's comment (cf. p. 38): "Miserable."
** Einstein's comment (he underlined the sentence): "Is that all?"

April 5, 1950

Mr. Ted O. Thackrey
The Daily Compass
New York, NY

Dear Ted:

You ask me to describe my experience with Dr. Harlow Shapley.

On April 13, 1946, four years ago, I met him at the Commodore Hotel, where he was a speaker at a College Forum discussing World Government. I asked whether he would give me a few minutes during the intermission. He graciously agreed. Here is our conversation almost to a word.

V.: Dr. Shapley, I was working for the last six years on a research and the results of it I have written down. In this research I came to the conclusion, certainly unorthodox, that in historical times there were changes in the constitution of the solar system.

I was careful not to say to Dr. Shapley what kind of changes, or when, they took place; neither did I mention the Old Testament or Joshua. Even in the book I mention Venus for the first time after page 150.

Sh.: How did you come to this conclusion?

V.: I worked mainly on ancient records, but I arrived to this conclusion also from other materials, geological ...

Sh.: (interrupting) Do you realize that we cannot build such a theory on an old record, which may be basically wrong?

V.: I did not build it on one record, but on many, from various races, from all corners of the world; from nations as far apart as Assyrians, Hindus, or the tribes of Mexico. The records corroborate one another.

Sh.: If so, then it is different. But do you realize that if there were, as you say, changes in the constitution of the solar system in historical times, your research must bring you into conflict with the Newtonian gravitation?

V. (thinking): Although my theory can be fitted into the prevailing Newtonian system, and actually small perturbations among planets and greater perturbations among comets occur regularly, perturbations of a magnitude that would change the orbits of the planets, are compatible with the Newtonian system of the world; and the idea of a planet between Mars and Jupiter, broken in some collision, was accepted long ago, without a conflict with Newton, etc ... but this Dr. Shapley must have a quick mind, since it is true that working on my book I wondered how it could be that a purely mechanistic theory survived in astronomy from the 17th century, and electricity and magnetism remained excluded from taking part in celestial motions; thus astronomy dogmatically defends the point that the earth and other planets, and comets, cannot be charged bodies, although geophysicists think that the earth is charged; and it has a magnetic field; and the comets have self-illuminating tails. The sun, that sends out a deluge of charged particles, must, as a whole, be also a neutral body, in order to keep the mechanistic system valid.

V. (aloud): Yes, I realized that. But in the present work I do not give any interpretation of the events described in terms of physics, I only try to establish facts. I wish you would agree to read the manuscript; and if you will be satisfied at its reading that my thesis is supported by sources to an extent that it deserves some laboratory investigation, would it be possible to undertake one or two rather not complicated spectroscopic analyses?

Sh.: I would like to read your manuscript, but I am very busy, and therefore if somebody whom I know would read it first and recommend it to me, I promise you to read it, too. And as to the experiments, write to me to the Harvard

cont'd

Velikovsky to Thackrey (cont'd)

> College Observatory, or to Dr. Whipple, my assistant, re-
> ferring to this our conversation, and if possible, we will do
> it for you.
>
> V.: I thank you, indeed. Whom would you suggest as the reader
> of my manuscript?
>
> Sh.: Do you know Professor Lynn Thorndike of Columbia?
>
> V.: I do not know him personally.
>
> Sh.: Ask him.
>
> V.: If Thorndike will not be able to attend to this, whom would
> you suggest?
>
> Sh.: Tell me some name.
>
> V.: How, for instance, Professor Horace Kallen? He read an-
> other manuscript of mine.
>
> Sh.: If Professor Kallen reads and recommends it, I shall care-
> fully read it, too.
>
> V.: I appreciate it, indeed.
>
> Sh.: I wish you luck. And believe me, if you have proved in
> your book that in historical times there occurred a change
> in the constitution of the solar system, there is nothing in
> my power that I would not do for you ...

Velikovsky thanked again Dr. Shapley, for the time he gave him and courtesy, and declining an invitation to stay for lunch, went home believing that he (V.) met a great and good man.

THE DAILY COMPASS
NEW YORK, NY

April 10, 1950

Dr. Harlow Shapley
Harvard College Observatory
Cambridge 38, Massachusetts

Dear Harlow:

I have delayed an answer to yours of March 8th until I could examine carefully some of the material to which your letter refers, and examine, as well, the circumstances under which it was written.

You refer to Science News Letter and to Time Magazine as evidences of unfavorable views of Dr. Velikovsky's work coinciding with your own, but unless I mistake certain reasonably clear indications, the chief inspiration for these adverse views, stems from Dr. Harlow Shapley of the Harvard College Observatory!

You note that you yourself are not writing anything in response to Dr. Velikovsky or Larrabee, and that, in fact, the only hot communication from you was your letter to me.

On the other hand, Mrs. Cecilia Payne-Gaposchkin's article was directly inspired by you, and I am informed by Mr. Gordon A. Atwater that two communications to Dr. Velikovsky's publishers, The Macmillan Company, from you, are so sizzling that your letter to me might seem tepid by comparison!

I do not doubt that many groups, including groups of Harvard University professors, who are by no means ill-mannered, injudicious or dumb – to quote you and agree with you on that score – hold views which coincide with your own; but I should be astonished to find that they had reached their conclusions completely independently of discussion with you.

cont'd

Thackrey to Shapley (cont'd)

There is, of course, a further elementary factor which continues to perplex and dismay me; at the time their views were expressed; at the time Dr. Gaposchkin's article was written, not you, nor Dr. Gaposchkin, nor the professors you cite – not one – had read the manuscript or the book. At most, they have read comment upon it, or digest of sections of it, without benefit of reference notes or complete treatment.

I am more than a little puzzled at your paragraph mentioning that "a vice-president of the American Astronomical Society thought that the Council of the Society should send a protest to Macmillan, the famous publisher of highly reputable scientific books; but I said immediately, and so did many others, that such an action would merely give greater publicity to Dr. Velikovsky's contributions. Freedom to publish is a basic freedom."

The reason for my bewilderment, in view of the foregoing paragraph, is that I have been assured that you yourself wrote on two separate occasions to Macmillan in an effort to frustrate publication of Dr. Velikovsky's work, and that in doing so your language was as severe as that in your original letter to me on the subject.

Would you please assure me that this report is wholly false; or if it is not, let me know how you would reconcile the paragraph I have quoted from your March 8th letter, and would you let me have copies of your letters?

I have, I believe, at least one advantage in this correspondence; and it is, indeed, not only an advantage in the exchange with you, but with Dr. Gaposchkin, and I suspect with the reviews of Dr. Velikovsky's book by Otto Struve in the April 2nd Book Review Section of the Herald-Tribune and by Waldemar Kaempffert, Science Editor of the Times, in that newspaper's April 2nd section. The advantage is that I have read the book in question, while I seriously doubt if you or the above named have actually done so as yet. In your own case, I am certain.

In the others, my suspicion lies in the language of the critical reviews due to certain errors of fact which would not be easy to misstate had the book or manuscript been examined.

The Struve review quotes directly from Dr. Gaposchkin's Reporter article, and has obviously been influenced by it. But it quotes, and Dr. Gaposchkin states as a fact, what is exceedingly doubtful, and that is the positive statement that the observations of Venus extend back to five hundred years before the Exodus "thus refuting the absurd story of a comet that turned into a planet."

If there is such an undisputed ancient observation of the existence of Venus as a planet on an orbit and with periods of revolution as they are at the present time, it would have been enlightening if both Dr. Gaposchkin and Struve had given the reference. They assume that in these tablets the movements of Venus are the same as today: they are not.

Kaempffert carries the matter further, and says, "If Venus did not become a planet until 1500 B.C. and therefore in historic times, ancient records should bear out Dr. Velikovsky," and proceeds to cite "the rising and setting of the planet" as recorded by King Ammizaduga and others, and refers to Langdon and Fotheringham's "The Venus Tablets," etc.

Then Kaempffert, falling into the same basic error as Dr. Gaposchkin and Struve – an error which does not require a mathematician or celestial mechanic to detect, goes on to make the amazing statement that "Dr. Velikovsky refers to these Venus tablets in a footnote but does not indicate their content!"

The facts can only show what a grievous error it is to write critically about unread material!

Dr. Velikovsky's book, pages 198 to 200, does not merely refer to the tablets in a footnote, but devotes two and one half pages of the text to indicating the content of the tablets, as outlined from various sources, including Langdon and Fotheringham (quoted by Kaempffert).

It would appear from the authorities cited by Velikovsky that there is a very considerable doubt indeed about the date of the tablets referred to in such an axiomatic way by Dr. Gaposchkin and Struve. Kaempffert places the tablets in the 16th century; Schiaparelli and F. Hommel referred them to the 8th-7th century B.C., but the most important fact is that these tablets of

cont'd

Thackrey to Shapley (cont'd)

Venus, of whatever time they originated, prove only that Venus then did not move as an orderly planet.

And it would definitely appear that the criticism that Dr. Velikovsky's book ignores the tablets except in a footnote could not have been written by anyone who read the book.

All this shows that you and Mrs. Gaposchkin made extensive and successful efforts to suppress the book, and damage it by statements not warranted by the text of the book. Into the same category belongs Gaposchkin's statement that Velikovsky confused Ovid and Hesiod. The confusion is hers.

I do not, myself, gain the impression from the book that Dr. Velikovsky feels patronizingly toward the scholars of Newton, Laplace, Lagrange, Newcomb or the great national observatories, nor that he wishes to scrap all preceding hypotheses, etc.

But it has filtered down through even the fog that surrounds my knowledge of scientific matters that there have been, from time to time, certain developments of the Newtonian theory, for example; since the time of its first utterance; refinements, if you will. Even Dr. Einstein has added a new mathematical formula to that which originally expressed his theory of relativity, but to examine it hardly means a complete repudiation of all that went before.

There is another matter about which I am curious: I am informed that Atwater has been asked to resign as curator of the planetarium here. Is it possible that your own reaction to his mild support of Dr. Velikovsky's right to publish could have influenced that decision?

I did note with interest that you feel that you are following the precedent of one Galileo; but I wonder if you would feel it unfair of me to remark that Galileo was advancing the thesis that the accepted science of his time was not yet perfected. I had thought it more likely that Dr. Velikovsky might fairly claim Galileo, as a precedent!

Sincerely,

(signed) Ted (T. O. Thackrey)

HARVARD COLLEGE OBSERVATORY
CAMBRIDGE, 38, MASS

June 6, 1950

Mr. T. O. Thackrey
The Daily Compass
164 Duane Street
New York 13, New York

Dear Ted:

To my letter of March 8 you replied on April 10. I should have written again on May 12, but I was then at our western observing stations.

I wonder if there is much point in writing further about Dr. V. and his remarkably successful writings. Certainly you and he and his publishers should be quite satisfied with his leadership of the best sellers for week after week, and I ought to be satisfied in that I have not yet met an astronomer or in fact a scientist or scholar of any sort, who takes "Worlds in Collision" seriously. Some referred to the clever promotion; some referred to the rather charming literary style; and some, while fully exonerating Dr. V. (who should do as he pleases in this free country), are unrestrained in their condemnation of the one reputable publisher. This point is made in many of the reviews.

In the annual address to an important scientific foundation, a distinguished American physiologist on Saturday bemoaned the rather black future, and obvious decadence of our times. We have failed completely in our scientific teaching, he stated, or the "Worlds in Collision" atrocity would not have caught on the way it has. It seemed to him that Dr. V. and Senator McCarthy are symbols of something dire and distressful. But I do not worry about it. Time has curative properties.

cont'd

Shapley to Thackrey (cont'd)

One thing did worry me a bit in your letter – your intimation that in some way I was carrying on a crusade against Dr. V. Of all the astronomers from whom I have heard comment, I am the mildest and most forgiving. You suggest directly that I am back of various hypothetical crusades, and that my letters to the Macmillan Company were scorchers. How you misjudge me! I enclose copies of the letter, also a copy of the letter from the president of the Macmillan Company. In rereading it seems to me that I am sad, but not savage.

Sincerely,

(Signed) Harlow

Thackrey to The Daily Compass

May 25, 1963

... Needless to say, I am thoroughly disgusted with Shapley's irresponsible attitude, and by no means agree that the Macmillan letters are harmless.

Sincerely,

(Signed) Ted Thackrey

Thackrey refused Shapley's request to print Payne-Gaposchkin's article, "Nonsense, Dr. Velikovsky," but it was later printed in *The Reporter*.

Velikovsky to Max Ascoli, The Reporter

March 1, 1950

Professor Max Ascoli:

My friends, Mr. John J. O'Neill of the Herald Tribune, G.A. Atwater, Director of Hayden Planetarium and Ted O. Thackrey of Daily Compass, called my attention to a piece by Mrs. Payne-Gaposchkin. The joint originators of this piece Shapley and Gaposchkin have tried also to suppress the publication of this book by writing to Macmillan, but to no avail.

None of these joint authors read a single page or line of my manuscript. Therefore, the analysis of the details of Worlds In Collision attempt to suppress the publication of the book (Shapley wrote to Macmillan that he will never buy a book from them), are certainly acts which do not appear well weighed, already because most of the arguments are met in the book, and would appear embarrassing to the writers of the article when the book will be published on April 3.

It would be good that, at least, the Editor of the magazine that will publish the article ("The Reporter") should acquaint himself with the text of the book.

What I expect is that first my theory will be branded as wrong; but when it will be accepted, it will be branded as not new.

It will be good and fair if you will supply the article by Gaposchkin with a note in which you would state that neither the editor nor the authors has read the book.

It was and is my conviction that the knowledge of the very probable large deposits of oil in Italy (a knowledge which I acquired from a manuscript of the tenth century, reprinted later) should not be given away to Standard Oil of New Jersey, interested in oil in Italy, nor to any other American or British Com-

cont'd

Velikovsky to Max Ascoli, The Reporter (cont'd)

pany. It would be disastrous for Italy if a large foreign company should become the owner of rich oil sources in Italy. In 1947 I offered to convey my information to the Minister of Commerce in the Italian Government; but I had no answer to my letter.

(Signed) Immanuel Velikovsky

Ascoli to Velikovsky

March 8, 1950

Dear Dr. Velikovsky:

This is to acknowledge your letter of March 1, and to let you know that *the editorial note you suggested we run with the Payne-Gaposchkin piece is not, in our opinion, necessary.*

(Signed) Max Ascoli

About the same time, Shapley recruited five scholars in different fields to denounce Velikovsky's theories in his own publication *Science News Letter*. And, a month later, he cited Payne-Gaposchkin's article in *Science News Letter*, urging all scientists to read her "scientific" refutation of *Worlds in Collision*. Shapley, Payne-Gaposchkin and Shapley's five critics from different fields did all of this without ever having read *Worlds in Collision*, which had not yet been published. These denunciations of Velikovsky's work were based on Payne-Gaposchkin's unscientific critique, which was only based on Larrabee's article in *Harper's*.

The opposition, lead by Harlow Shapley, had escalated its war against Velikovsky. Otto Struve, director of the Yerkes Observatory at the University of Chicago and ex-president of the American Astronomical Society, joined the letter-writing campaign. He wrote to John O'Neill, science editor of the Herald Tribune, and to Gordon Atwater, chairman of the Department of Astronomy at the Museum of Natural History. He asked that they cease their support of Velikovsky and his work. Both refused to comply with Struve's request. Atwater replied that although he did not agree with everything Velikovsky wrote, he believed it had great value for the scientific world.

Otto Struve to Harper's

THE UNIVERSITY OF CHICAGO
YERKES OBSERVATORY
WILLIAMS BAY, WIS

March 3, 1950

The Editor
Harper's Magazine
49 East 33rd Street
New York 16, N.Y.

Dear Sir:

You have undoubtedly received numerous letters from astronomers who have objected to the contents of the article on the theory of Mr. Velikovsky which appeared in a recent issue of your magazine. I would like to add my voice to those of my colleagues. I am afraid that you have rendered a disservice to America and to science by publishing this altogether unsound article. In doing so you have furnished ammunition to our enemies in the Soviet Union and elsewhere; they are trying to prove that American scientists confuse religious issues with

cont'd

matters of science and are misleading the people by presenting to them false theories for the purpose of creating an idealistic outlook based upon faith rather than cold logic. When I read your article I was in the process of collecting material to expose and refute some of these Russian arguments, but I am beginning to wonder whether there is not a grain of truth to their criticism. Undoubtedly many ordinary people who have no means for ascertaining the truth will be misled by this extraordinary mixture of scientific nonsense and wishful thinking.

There is no excuse for going back to the kind of science the world had 1000 years ago. The claims of pseudo-scientists that the professional workers are prejudiced and unwilling to listen to new ideas are, I am afraid, reactionary in character and will cause no end of harm. Will you not make some effort to correct this situation either by printing a series of statements by competent scientists, or by asking some reputable person to prepare an article on what the best informed astronomers really think about the past history of the earth, the sun and the stars?

Very truly yours,

(Signed) Otto Struve

THE DAILY COMPASS
NEW YORK, NY

November 24, 1950

Dear Mr. Stephens,

I am unable to see eye to eye with you on the statement that Velikovsky's work is a hindrance to the cause of learning rather than a help. I, perhaps, am the only one who has had opportunity to become acquainted with Velikovsky's complete works.

Dr. Shapley causes members of the Observatory staff to write letters to me urging withdrawal of support for the book and uniting in an effort to bring about its suppression. Many others received such letters. He urges astronomers in other observatories to write such letters.

In addition, he starts a campaign in the schools and colleges to boycott Macmillan's educational books (their major sales item) unless Velikovsky's book was suppressed. His campaign was successful. James Putnam, Macmillan's editor for 25 years, was dismissed. Gordon Atwater, Director of the Hayden Planetarium at the American Museum of Natural History, wrote a non-committal magazine article on the book and almost immediately his resignation was asked for ...

I offered to write a review of the book for my paper and would have written a well-balanced article giving the pros and cons. The offer was declined. *The book was given for review to Dr. Otto Struve. Dr. Struve, at the behest of Dr. Shapley, had previously written a letter to me asking me to withdraw support and aid in suppressing the book.*

This campaign by Dr. Shapley does violence to my concept of freedom of speech and of the fundamentals of our American democracy and of ethical behavior.

(Signed) John J. O'Neill

Despite these negative reviews, the public loved *Worlds in Collision*, and it remained on the best-seller fist of the *New York Times* and the *Herald Tribune*. However, on May 25, 1950, the pressure from the Shapleyites was mounting on George Brett, president of Macmillan Publishing. He asked that my father come to meet with him. At that meeting Brett expressed his concern over the violent opposition from the members of the scientific establishment and the threat of a boycott of Macmillan's textbooks (Their textbook sales comprised 70% of total revenue). He said that never in his thirty-three years in publishing did he have to ask an author to release his publishing company from a contract. Then, he asked my father to do just this. He explained that he had found another publisher, Doubleday Company, that agreed to publish *Worlds in Collision*. After careful consideration, my father agreed to go with Doubleday. Soon after the transfer took place, James Putnam, my father's editor, was terminated by Macmillan.

Years later, Harold S. Latham, chief editor of Macmillan Publishing would write, in his book *My Life in Publishing* (1965), that he always felt regret over Brett's decision. In 1965, Latham wrote a letter to Velikovsky saying that

> I remember well the commotion caused by *Worlds in Collision* and I do not remember with any pleasure the part that Macmillan played in the episode. I always felt that we made a mistake in taking so seriously the criticisms and demands of the scientists and textbook authors.
>
> I should have preferred to stand our ground and face our detractors and I think they might very soon have been put to the rout. But the decision was not mine to make.

Harold Latham inscribed his book *My Life in Publishing*:

> For Immanuel Velikovsky with the esteem and best wishes of the author – Harold S. Latham

On p. 75 he wrote:

> It has long been a source of regret to me that Macmillan followed the course it did in this matter. I have felt that we should have stood our ground ... This tale has a significant aftermath. Much of the controversy about *Worlds in Collision* centered around the question: How hot is Venus. Dr. Velikovsky advanced the theory – decried by scientists in general – that the surface of Venus must be very hot and that the atmosphere around the planet contained hydrocarbons or petroleum gas. The author was not, however, per-

mitted to try to prove or disprove this thinking, for the observatories where he sought to make tests refused him permission and called his ideas surprising and absurd. **Now comes the payoff!** Mariner II, ... was launched in August and sent toward Venus ... according to its findings the surface temperature of Venus is about 800 degrees Fahrenheit and that high above the planet's surface is a cover, about fifteen miles thick, composed of hydrocarbons ...

Shapley to Latham

HARVARD COLLEGE OBSERVATORY
CAMBRIDGE, MASS.

July 7, 1950

Mr. H.S. Latham
The Macmillan Company

Dear Mr. Latham,

I acknowledge the receipt of your letter of June 8, 1950. The several astronomers to whom a similar letter was sent talked extensively of this action of The Macmillan Company when they met at the University of Indiana two weeks ago. At that meeting I discovered that the protest by some of my colleagues at the Harvard Observatory were mild compared with the protests of many of the mid-west scientists. In fact it turned out to be the calmest of any, notwithstanding the elaborate attempts in New York City to indicate a conspiracy led by me!

I should like to add, confidentially, except perhaps for Mr. Brett, that it was my personal objection and opposition that prevented the American Astronomical Society from publicizing the unanimous action of its council (of which you of course know). Both the action of the Council and a petition from prominent members were sent (so far as I know) and largely because of your letter of June 8 and my personal protest. Nothing has stirred the astronomers and astrophysicists and physicists so much for quite a time. I regret they took the matter so seriously.

Sincerely yours,

(Signed) Harlow Shapley

The relentless attempts at suppressing Velikovsky's work did not stop after Macmillan Company transferred *Worlds in Collision* to Doubleday Company. On June 30, 1950, Fred Whipple, Shapley's successor as director at the Harvard Observatory, wrote to Eunice Stevens, associate editor of the Blakiston Company.

Whipple to Stevens

HARVARD COLLEGE OBSERVATORY
CAMBRIDGE, MASS

June 30, 1950

Mrs. Eunice Stevens,
Associate Editor
THE BLAKISTON COMPANY

Dear Mrs. Stevens:

Only in the last few days did I hear that the Doubleday Company had taken over the "golden chestnut" called WORLDS IN COLLISION by Velikovsky. The spontaneous boycott of the Macmillan Company arose, not from an effort at suppression of the book, but as a protest against misrepresentation of a manufactured article. There would not have been the slightest stir among the scientists had this book been labeled properly as fiction, instead it was touted as a great contribution to science with a large amount of ballyhoo. The fact that the book was scientific rot being perpetrated on an unsuspecting public appears never to have touched the conscience of the Macmillan Company. If this distinction between fiction and nonfiction sounds trivial to you, I ask you to consider how many volumes would have been sold had the book come out under its proper designation as fiction.

Scientists have no objections to the publication of crank literature so long as it is not presented by reputable publishers as

---

a scientific contribution. The situation is similar to many covered by the Food and Drug Act. No one objects to a manufacturer selling pure white sand so long as he labels it pure white sand. If he puts it into a container and calls it salt, then, of course, he is considered a criminal.

Velikovsky differs from other crank scientific writers in that he has the art of making the impossible seem plausible. It is conceivable, but highly unlikely, that the Macmillan Company was actually led astray by this high degree of plausibility. Hence, the position of the Doubleday Company in buying the rights to WC represents a considerably lower ethical level than that of the Macmillan Company, since the Doubleday Company cannot have avoided obtaining the opinion of many competent scientists. Oddly enough, in its anti-scientific account of the book, *Newsweek* has unwittingly done the Doubleday Company a considerable amount of harm. They have made public the high success of the spontaneous boycott of the Macmillan Company by scientifically minded people. This in turn amounts to organizing a boycott of the Doubleday Company by the thinking people who buy books. My guess is that the Doubleday Company will never publish Volumes 3 and 4. They will discover, in my opinion, as Macmillan has already undoubtedly discovered, that the writers of books are thinking people of high standards. In any case, since I believe that the Blakiston Company is owned by the Doubleday Company, which controls its policies as well as the distribution of its books, I am now then a fellow author of the Doubleday Company along with Velikovsky. My natural inclination, were it possible, is to take EARTH, MOON AND PLANETS off the market and find a publisher who is not associated with one who has such a lacuna in its publication ethics. This is not possible, however, so the next best that I can do is to turn over future royalty checks to the Boston Community Fund and to let EARTH, MOON AND PLANETS die of senescence. In other words, there will be no revision of EARTH, MOON AND PLANETS forthcoming so long as Doubleday owns Blakiston, controls its policies and publishes WORLDS IN COLLISION.

cont'd

Whipple to Stevens (cont'd)

It is with deep regret that I write this letter and with regret that your fine company has become financially associated with a company which appears to lack ethics in its publication practices.

I very much hope that you can prove to me that I am misinformed in some details.

Sincerely yours,

(Signed) Fred L. Whipple
Chairman
Department of Astronomy

McCormick to Whipple

July 18, 1950

Mr. Fred L. Whipple, Chairman
Department of Astronomy
Harvard College Observatory

Dear Dr. Whipple:

Mrs. Stevens of the Blakiston Company has sent me a copy of your recent letter to her, which has upset her very much. We at Doubleday are also distressed that our editorial policy has disturbed you.

Before explaining our position, however, it must be pointed out categorically that although Doubleday & Company does own the Blakiston Company, it exercises no control of or influence on Blakiston's editorial policy. *The Blakiston Company operates independently and so does Doubleday, so much so that Mrs. Stevens did not know we have taken over the publication of WORLDS IN COLLISION until sometime after the fact.*

We took over the publication of Professor Velikovsky's book because there was great demand for it and we believe that the book business cannot let itself be pressured into censorship. You know, better than I, how much important work would have been lost to the world if such were the custom. When Doubleday took the book, WORLDS IN COLLISION had already had a public trial, it had been widely reviewed and discussed in the public press, receiving both condemnation and commendation. We have not forced the book on anyone nor do we offer it as a textbook. In no way do we present it as "a great contribution to science," as you suggest, but as one man's personal theory.

In our advertisements we have billed WORLDS IN COLLISION only as a controversial book, quoting the varying opinions of prominent writers, scientists, statesmen, and reviewers, and presenting the pros and cons with no implication that either side was right.

We can understand that scientists feel bound to challenge Professor Velikovsky; but *we contend that the way to disprove his theory is not to ban his book or boycott his publishers, but to answer him. If any of the scientists aroused by this book, will present a counter-argument in a manuscript as interesting, Doubleday will be very glad to consider it for publication.*

I hope very much that you will revise your opinion of the editorial ethics of Doubleday & Company and endeavor to see that, from our point of view, there are ethics involved in protecting the right of a man to have a hearing and keeping the publishing business free for the expression of ideas.

Sincerely,

(Signed) Ken McCormick
Editor-in-Chief
Doubleday and Company, Inc.

On July 2, 1970, Whipple later denied his letter when he told Clark Whelton of *The Village Voice*:

> With regard to Dr. Velikovsky's "Worlds In Collision" there is no change in my attitude or in the situation since the book was first released nearly a decade (sic) ago. There is no truth to allegations that I sought to dissuade the Doubleday Company from publishing this book or any other book ...
>
> (Kallen, 1976, p.25)

Cressey to Doubleday

SYRACUSE UNIVERSITY
SYRACUSE, NEW YORK
Department of Geology

June 26, 1950

Doubleday & Company, Inc.

Gentlemen:

I am concerned over the fact that you have taken over the publication of Velikovsky's "Worlds In Collision" from Macmillan. It seems to me that publishers have a moral responsibility to assure their readers that their publications carry an essential element of authority and honesty.

I cannot write as an astronomer, but as a geologist I am at least able to recognize the gross inaccuracies in Velikovsky's book. You may make some money by adding his title to your list, but you surely impair your reputation with the informed public.

Sincerely yours,

George B. Cressey

Cc: Macmillan

AMHERST COLLEGE
AMHERST, MA
Department of Chemistry

June 23, 1950

Doubleday & Company, Inc.

Gentlemen:

I note from Time magazine that your firm has taken over the publication of Velikovsky's "Worlds In Collision" and I wish to register protest against the further printing of this work. It is scientific charlatanism of the worst sort and does no credit to any publishing house. Macmillan Company abandoned it because of the storm of protest it aroused among informed persons, and you, too, may find yourself kept busy answering letters of indignation from scientists the country over.

Scientists are now engaged in an active boycott of the Macmillan books, and though scientists are not important buyers of your books and their opinion should be heeded by any publisher who intends to publish a book which purports to be science. I trust that you can be dissuaded.

Very truly yours,

(Signed) David C. Grahame
Associate Professor of Chemistry

P.S. It doesn't seem to me to be fair play to capitalize upon the ignorance of the People in matters of science. And at the scientists' expense, I might add.

THE DAILY COMPASS
NEW YORK, NY

July 10, 1950

Dr. David C. Grahame
Associate Professor Chemistry
Amherst College
Amherst, Mass.

Dear Dr. Grahame:

Thank you for writing us concerning Immanuel Velikovsky's WORLDS IN COLLISION. We were interested in your letter and glad to have an expression of your opinion.

Our reason for taking over the publication of Professor Velikovsky's book is that we believe that in this country it is important that opinions are expressed and not suppressed. Book publishing is one of the great strongholds of free speech, and Doubleday believes actively in this academic freedom. We have published many books of diverse views and hope to continue to do so. Until now we have not been threatened with organized boycott.

WORLDS IN COLLISION has had a public trial. It has not been forced on anyone, nor is it offered as a textbook. Review copies were sent to all regular media, and the book has received its criticism publicly, both of condemnation and commendation.

We have respect for your challenge to Professor Velikovsky's theories and if any of your group wishes to present his contrary views in a manuscript, equally as interesting, we shall be very glad to consider it for publication.

Sincerely,

(Signed) Louise Thomas
Doubleday

July 27, 1950

Mr. Ken McCormick
Chief Editor
Doubleday and Company, Inc.
14 West 49th Street
New York, New York

Dear Mr. McCormick:

I am in possession of the copies of the letter written by you to Dr. Whipple of Harvard College Observatory in reply to his letter to Mrs. Stevens of the Blakiston Company in Philadelphia and also of the letter by Mr. Cressey from Syracuse University, Department of Geography, and your reply to him. I am grateful to you for lending me these copies as well as the earlier copy of the letter of Mr. Grahame, a chemist at Amherst, and the answer to him by Mrs. Louise Thomas. Thankful as I am to you for letting me see this correspondence, I do not think that these gentlemen received the answers that they deserved.

Dr. Whipple says that "the position of the Doubleday Company in buying the rights to 'Worlds in Collision' represents a considerably lower ethical level than that of the Macmillan Company" because you were aware of what you were doing. He writes his letter after he read an article in Newsweek, "Professors as Suppressors." I believe that, acting now as he does, he stoops to a lower ethical level than when he and his colleagues of Harvard College Observatory tried to suppress the book at Macmillan because, from this article of Newsweek and from editorials in various publications, he must know by now the definition of what he is doing.

In the same article in Newsweek referred to in the letter of Dr. Whipple, it is said: "Dr. Shapley denied heatedly that he conducted any kind of campaign against the book. Nor had the Harvard College Observatory, he added. He did write Macmillan about the book and so did other members of the observatory

cont'd

but again, 'I did not make any threats and I don't know anyone who did.'"

In the brief of Dr. Whipple to the Blakiston Company, he makes the threat that "there will be no edition of 'Earth, Moon and Planets' forthcoming so long as Doubleday owns Blakiston, controls its policies and publishes 'Worlds in Collision'." He finished by accusing Doubleday of lack of ethics.

To prove his point that the book has no scientific value, is "rot" and a piece of "crank literature", he says only that "Velikovsky has the art of asking the impossible seem plausible" and adds, "I must say that in areas of the book where I am not fully informed the writing seems almost convincing." He does not bring any instance of a wrong statement in my book in the field of astronomy or anywhere else; and actually despite many efforts on the part of his associate at Harvard College Observatory, Mrs. Cecilia Payne-Gaposchkin, in her recent long article in the Popular Astronomy, she could not bring one valid physical or astronomical argument against the book and tries to refute a few single literary items of the book in a way which discloses bar ignorance in the field.

I believe I do not need to dwell upon all this since you have read the book and you accepted it not only because "there is a public demand for it" but also because, in your own judgment, it is a book worth publication which you intend to do with pride. You write to Dr. Whipple that "Mrs. Stevens of the Blakiston Company was very much upset by (his) letter to her" and that "we at Doubleday are also distressed that our editorial policy has disturbed you." By this you only invite more letters of the scientists from different places which are in some contact with the members of the Harvard College Observatory.

I regard my publisher not as a place of refuge and shelter from the fury of attacking scientists but as a bastion for the propagation of my literary or scientific efforts. In this connection, you will be interested to see the correspondence between Mr. McLaughlin and Fulton Oursler, and also a copy of an editorial from the Columbus Ohio Dispatch as an example of editorials that appeared in connection with the suppression of my book.

As to the new edition of Whipple's "Earth, Moon and Planets," I do not believe that in one or two years from now it would be possible without incorporating into it the historical facts documented in "Worlds in Collision." This Dr. Whipple, however, may keep his name for posterity, not by his scientific discoveries, if he has any, but by his letters that, as the earlier letters from Shapley and his associates, in the opinion of my lawyer, have all the signs of conspiracy.

I had to let this off my chest since I know that Ken McCormick is an editor of high principles, without compare.

Cordially yours,

(Signed) Velikovsky

P.S. This Monday, I was, by invitation, the guest of the President and the members of the faculties of Bridgeport University. They made me feel that they are entirely on my side. I also received letters from Professor Tyler, retired Acting Dean, School of Mines, Pittsburgh; Professor Miller, Professor of Physics, Dillard University in New Orleans; Professor V. Komarewsky, Illinois Institute of Technology; and Professor Jacobs of Bridgeport University; the attitude of all of them is diametrically opposed to that of Dr. Whipple, Cressey of Syracuse and Grahame of Amherst.

THE OBSERVATORY OF THE
UNIVERSITY OF MICHIGAN
ANN ARBOR, MICHIGAN

June 18, 1950

Mr. Fulton Oursler

Dear Mr. Oursler:

Several days ago I read your article "The Twilight of Honor" in the June issue of Reader's Digest.

Let me assure you I am not in the habit of writing letters to attempt to convert people whose views differ from mine. The present occasion is a very special one; the first in twenty years, I believe, if we omit criticisms of the views of some of my scientific colleagues who themselves requested criticism. My reason for writing to you at this time is that you had a part in advancing to the best-seller category a book that scientists confidently appraise as mere rubbish and the most flagrant intellectual fraud ever foisted upon the public.

To put it bluntly, for which I apologize, your one article earnestly attacks dishonesty, and your review applauds it! I fully realize that you were not then aware of the true character of Velikovsky's book and that, like many other people untrained in science, you were (shall I say) "taken in".

Scientists are the first to admit the limitations of their knowledge. But, we are aware (by objective tests) of which sections are certain, which are only probable and which extremely uncertain. The Velikovsky book is not concerned with questions that lie at the very frontier of knowledge (where admittedly anything can happen), but with matters that have satisfied very thorough and highly exact tests of agreement between calculation (theory) and observation.

One could write a voluminous book presenting all the facts and completely demolish Velikovsky's thesis. I doubt that any scientist or group of them will waste their time that way.

I find it difficult to believe the author sincere, yet the circumstances confirm such belief. He appears to be completely deluded and incapable of assessing facts in an objective way. Many of the "facts" he uses to bolster his views are fabrications from legends so vague that they could mean nearly anything one wished.

One thing that is most astonishing is your uncritical approach.

Most of all it is hard to see why you were not suspicious of his claims to such extensive knowledge. Whenever a man claims to "know everything," and especially when he makes sweeping statements dismissing the competence of many experts, be sure he is a quack. Remember the old patent-medicine man whose medicine "cured everything"!

Here I am talking to you like the proverbial "Dutch uncle"! I hate to adopt an attitude of "I know and you don't." Please understand that I am speaking for a great number of experts collectively. On another subject, our positions could easily be reversed! If his were merely a crackpot book about astronomy I would just laugh it off. But it is worse than that; worse than an attack on science; it is an attack on reason; especially it is a boomerang attack on religion!

Many religious people are "falling for" this crazy "theory". But what they do not see is this: if the Biblical miracles are explained as mere natural phenomena or explained by Velikovsky's "science", then they are no longer miracles; we then have merely science and no religion at all! This is no solution. The conflict will not be resolved by clutching at Velikovsky's straw.

All of us who write have a very genuine responsibility to the public. We must be honest and responsible; and here we are back to "The Twilight of Honor." To be honest and responsible, we must be self-critical. By being uncritical you, unintentionally, aided and abetted dishonesty and irresponsibility. I refer to the publisher of the book. Their responsibility was clear; they should not mislead the public. They could have consulted experts in the various fields of science, but they did not. Similarly, you could have consulted experts, but did not.

cont'd

McLaughlin to Fulton Oursler (cont'd)

Experts of course can be wrong. We have to take that risk. But the public needs to recognize that expertness can and does exist, and that experts, by and large, are our best risk.

"Worlds In Collision" has just changed hands from Macmillan to Doubleday. I am frank to state that this change was the result of pressure that scientists and scholars brought to bear on the Macmillan Company. It is our duty to the public to prevent such frauds insofar as we can. But the transfer merely means that the first publisher has "saved face" and the fraud can still go on. It is our belief that freedom of the press is abused when the public can be widely misinformed by the elevation of such a book to the bestseller class. The payment of royalties and the reaping of profit from a book like "Worlds In Collision" do indeed mark "The Twilight of Honor."

Yours very sincerely,

(Signed) Dean B. McLaughlin
Professor of Astronomy

THE READER'S DIGEST
PLEASANTVILLE, N.Y.

June 27, 1950

Dear Professor McLaughlin:

I appreciate the long and thoughtful letter that you wrote me although I find some parts of it difficult to understand.

One part has to do with the pride you express in the pressure of scientists against the house of Macmillan to discontinue publishing the Velikovsky book. This procedure horrifies me; some of the details of which I have been told are witch-hunting tactics. Is not this book-burning by intellectuals? And isn't that a matter for shame rather than pride? This, above all in your letter, I cannot understand.

You say that my article on the Twilight of Honor aroused your admiration but that your views of it were strongly discolored by my review of Worlds in Collision.

I cannot understand why you should suggest that there was anything dishonorable in my review. It was an honest report of a book that certainly had made news.

Again you state that my review applauds dishonesty. Do you consider that remark an example of objective scientific observation? To use your own words, that comment of yours is "mere rubbish and a flagrant intellectual fraud." Because you know perfectly well that my review does not applaud dishonesty. This, you yourself realize and apologize for it in your next paragraph. I mention it here only to point out that a serious discussion should be conducted in less extravagant and emotional terms.

You go on to say that scientists admit the limitations of their knowledge but are aware of which sections are certain, which are only probable and which extremely uncertain.

I hold no brief whatever for Dr. Velikovsky or for his thesis. The three "facts" which you mention may be very important.

cont'd

But merely because you have stated them to me, I cannot condemn Dr. Velikovsky without a hearing. I am bringing them to his attention and asking him how he would explain the apparent discrepancies.

I think it pertinent to ask if you have also asked him the same questions.

You talk now of Velikovsky as Pasteur's critics talked of him in other days. I do not compare Velikovsky with Pasteur. But I am astonished at your emotion as reflected in your language.

You are quite right in saying that you talk to me like a Dutch uncle and I am sure you will not deny me the privilege of talking back to you like an American uncle. Therefore I must point out to you that when you ask me to believe that Velikovsky's "science" vitiates the Biblical miracles you are very far from the truth. Let me remind you of your own remarks to beware of a man who claims to know everything. Aren't you dangerously near to doing that at this point? There is nothing in Velikovsky's theory that removes the miraculous intervention of God at just the right time, in full accord with the Biblical position; at least that is the point of view of some of the theologians with whom I discussed the matter.

I am sufficiently interested in what you say to take your letter to Dr. Velikovsky and hear what he has to say about it.

Sincerely yours,

(Signed) Fulton Oursler
Senior Editor

P.S.: Is it true that this agitation among scientists originated with Professor Harlow Shapley? If so, I am bound to regard these hysterical attitudes and attempts at book burnings in a light even more dubious.

July 6, 1950

Mr. Fulton Oursler
The Reader's Digest
NewYork, NY

Dear Mr. Oursler:

It was very kind of you to write to me and it was wise to include the letter of McLaughlin of Ann Arbor.

You will best understand his moral and intellectual quality if I disclose to you that on May 25th Mr. Brett, the president of Macmillan, gave me to read, and to make notes from, a letter addressed to Macmillan, dated May 20th, from this same Mc-Laughlin. In that long letter, Dean B. McLaughlin wrote that my book consists of *"lies yes, only lies"; and on the lower part of the same page he wrote, "I have not read the book – no – I will never read the book."* Therefore, his assertion to you that he could write a full book about my book is a vain boast.

He accuses me of fraud and professes in his letter that "we must be honest and responsible." Is it honest and responsible to write as he did to you about a book he did not read, leaving you with the impression that he had studied it? One of the prominent lawyers in this country finds that what he is actually doing is making himself guilty of libel, blackmail and conspiracy.

I don't think it is wise to answer the criticism of somebody who has not read the book and proclaimed that he would never read it. Nevertheless, in order that you, who previewed my book in The Reader's Digest, should feel assured that up till now no valid scientific argument has been published by the opponents of the book, I want to say, in short, that –

1) Venus, as a planet on a regular orbit, was not mentioned in any document prior to the eighth century or even seventh century before the present era. The argument of the early tablets of Venus was first used by Mrs. Gaposchkin, the assistant of Shapley, in the "Reporter" of March 14th. Four weeks later, in the "Reporter" of April 11th, however, in answering Mr. Larrabee

cont'd

Velikovsky to Fulton Oursler (cont'd)

who wrote to the editor of the "Reporter" protesting that *Mrs. Gaposchkin* analyzed and rejected the book on the basis of his short preview in Harper's, she *admitted that she had not read the book when she wrote her article. Professor Shapley* gave her article a wide circulation. However, in a correspondence with Mr. Ted Thackrey, editor of the Daily Compass, he *tacitly admitted that he, too, had not read the book.*

The same argument of the Babylonian Venus tablets was repeated by both Kaempffert and Struve, and I replied to Kaempffert in a letter published by the New York Times Book Review Section (a copy of which I enclose). The document in question (the Venus Tablets of Ammizaduga) describes movements of Venus which are inconsistent with its being a planet and prove that at the time of the document, Venus moved as a comet. Schiaparelli and Hommel, as I showed in my book on pp. 198-200, referred these tablets to the eighth or seventh century before the present era, but if they originated, as Kugler thought, in the first Babylonian dynasty, and Kaempffert, following Neugebauer, referred them to the sixteenth century B. C., then the conclusion would be only that already at that time, Venus was a comet.

2) McLaughlin asserts that the observation of solar eclipses in precise times and places date back to 2,137 B. C. Mrs. Gaposchkin, in a more recent article in "Popular Astronomy," (in which she asserts that this time she read the book), says that the observation of solar eclipses dates hack to 1062 B. C. The truth is that most ancient solar eclipses, the dates of which are established, are those which are found, mostly in Claudius Ptolemy and no precise dates of eclipses are known from any document prior to the beginning of the seventh century.

A few references to eclipses or other apparent disturbances of the sun are given in older sources. However, the dates are not known and are calculated with the help of modern reckoning of the times when and where eclipses are expected to have happened. Even for historical eclipses after 700 B. C., the exact dates are not established. Thus, the date of the most famous eclipse of Antiquity which was presaged by Thales and occurred during the battle of Alyattes the Lydian and Cyaxares the Median, is still debated and referred differently to May 28,

585 B. C., and September 30, 610 B. C. The earlier eclipses are arbitrarily referred to the dates when they are expected to have happened.

One English scholar calculated once that the solar and lunar eclipses prove that since thousands of years, there is a delay of 1/1000 of a second in a century in the lunar eclipses. This, of course, is scholarship of the kind of the notorious pyramidal inch. How can we know with exactitude the hour, minute and second of the observations of the ancients? However, this theory was taken for its face value by astronomers who draw their conclusions as to the retarding tidal action (friction) on the moon and this argument was also brought by Harvard professors against me. However, it was quickly dropped because what my opponents from the camp of exact scientists tried to prove is that historical documents have very little value and my book is full of historical documents. Therefore they would no more insist on such precision in ancient observations and testimonies.

3) The problem of changing the direction of the world's cardinal points is discussed at large in my "Worlds in Collision" and the orientation of ancient temples, the ancient charts and inscriptions, water clocks, sundials and the reforms of calendar are discussed there at great length. The azimuths of various pyramids, as well as the purpose of the pyramids and the effects of earth shocks on them, will be discussed in detail in that volume of my work which will deal with the earlier catastrophes that occurred before the end of the Middle Kingdom in Egypt.

I trust that this is satisfactory to you. Perhaps sometime you would ask McLaughlin to send you a copy of his letter of May 20th to Macmillan's. He certainly should not be reluctant to send it to you since he is so proud of it.

And now that the book that you reviewed in The Reader's Digest has become an object of debate and has an unusual fate, I remember your prediction in this regard. However, did you also expect such a fury of controversy, accusations and misrepresentations?

Sincerely yours,

(Signed) Velikovsky

Velikovsky to George Sokolsky

August 1, 1950

Dear Mr. Sokolsky:

In your column of July 26th (The New York Post) you quote Professor Herget of Cincinnati who wrote to you, "You are certainly a fraud, writing such a long column on something you have not read or investigated." He refers to your article of July 7th on burning of books in which you stated that you have not read "Worlds in Collision", know it only by a condensation in *Collier's*, do not express an opinion of the work, however object to the censorship and the practice of suppression.

May I comment on this observation of the astronomer from Cincinnati? The opposition to my book was started soon after a preview by E. Larrabee, one of the editors of *Harper's Magazine*, appeared in its January issue. On February 25th in *Science News Letter*, of which H. Shapley of Harvard College Observatory is the president, he let it be printed that (he) was speaking for (his) fellow astronomers "and that Dr. Velikovsky's book is rubbish and nonsense." On March 8th, he admitted, in answer to a publisher of a daily in New York, that he had not seen "Worlds in Collision."

A professor of astronomy from Ann Arbor wrote to the president of Macmillan on May 25th: "'Worlds in Collision' consists of lies, yes only lies." He underlined these words and on the same page he wrote, "I have not read the book, no I will never read it", and he underlined the words again. And he was one of those who announced a boycott of Macmillan textbooks.

You, Mr. Sokolsky, are accused of being a "fraud" for admitting of not having read but a piece in Collier's, though you have not discussed the content or the value of the book, but only defended the freedom of publication. What to say about these three astronomers who admittedly had not read the book at the time they announced their verdict in the press?

Very sincerely yours,

(Signed) Velikovsky

November 10, 1950

Editor
The Harvard Crimson

Dear Sir:

A copy of the registration number of your publication came into my hands. It contains the following statement by Professor Shapley: "The claim that Dr. Velikovsky's book is being suppressed is nothing but a publicity promotion stunt. Like having a book banned in Boston, it improves the sales. Several attempts have been made to link such a move to stop the book's publication to some organization or to the Harvard Observatory. This idea is absolutely false."
I wonder how this statement can square with the fact that Professor Shapley was the first to write to Macmillan Company asking them not to proceed with the publication of the book. He wrote on January 18 and January 25, long before the book was published, and at a time when he had not read a single page of the book. I challenge him to publish in full these two very vehement letters, copies of which are in my possession, as well as his very unusual correspondence with Ted O. Thackrey, of the Daily Compass, in which Thackrey accuses him of acting criminally. *How, further can his statement that nobody of the Harvard Observatory made any effort to harm or suppress the publication of "Worlds in Collision" be squared with the letter of his assistant, Professor Fred L. Whipple, to the Blakiston Company, Philadelphia, a subsidiary of Doubleday, who took over the book from Macmillan, should stop its publication under the threat that no new edition of his work would be published by Blakiston and that he would also refuse any further royalties for his Earth, Moon and Planets.* How, furthermore, can the statement of Professor Shapley be squared with the fact that, at his initiative, Mrs. Cecilia Payne-Gaposchkin, another assistant of his, wrote "Nonsense, Dr. Velikovsky" for the Reporter, and before its publication circulated her article from the Harvard Observa-

cont'd

Velikovsky to The Harvard Crimson (cont'd)

tory in mimeographed form among many scientific reviewers of daily and weekly publications in this country at a time when "Worlds in Collision" was not yet published? Mrs. Payne-Gaposchkin admitted in a letter to the Reporter on April 11, which was in answer to a letter from Eric Larrabee of Harper's, that she had not read the book when she wrote and published and circulated her article in the Reporter on March 14.

These three facts must be denied and proved to be fiction before the statements of Professor Shapley in the Harvard Crimson, in which he denies having caused me any moral or material harm, and also previously in Newsweek of July 3 (*"... Dr. Shapley last week denied heatedly that he conducted any campaign against the book: ... 'I didn't make any threats and I don't know anyone who did.'"*).

Very sincerely yours,

(Signed) Velikovsky

Gordon D. Atwater, Curator of the Hayden Planetarium and in 1950, Director of the Department of Astronomy at the American Museum of Natural History, was one of the readers of the manuscript of *Worlds in Collision* for Macmillan. He also planned a dramatization of the events in the book and prepared a review that was critical but not unfavorable. As a result of these activities, he lost both his positions. However, an article he wrote still appeared in the April 2nd issue of *This Week*, a magazine published by the *Herald Tribune*. Although the editors felt the pressure not to print it, John O'Neill, after showing them Payne-Gaposchkin's mimeographed article, advised them to print Atwater's article. In it, Atwater wrote that *Worlds in Collision* will have an explosive effect in the world of science, and while the book "is being condemned by large numbers of professional scientists, many other groups will welcome the book as a broadening influence in scientific, religious and philosophical fields (printed in *Stargazers and Gravediggers*, File I, »The Book Is Launched, Atwater Thrown Overboard«)." O'Neill had also composed a review of *Worlds in Collision* for the same April 2nd issue (the day before publication and release of the book), but it was replaced with a review by none other than Otto Struve. Instead of presenting an objective, scientific critical analysis of *Worlds in Collision*, Struve offered an unscientific rejection of it with not a shred of data to support that rejection. His excuse was that because *Worlds in Collision* was not a book of science he did not have to analyze it on the basis of scientific terms. (This tactic, to dismiss Velikovsky's work as unscientific, has been continually used by the scientific establishment until the present day, most likely to keep Velikovsky's theories outside of the realm of science, where they might actually be discovered to be accurate.) Struve, instead, chose to cite what he considered to be a scientific work, Cecilia Payne-Gaposchkin's article in *The Reporter*, which misrepresented Velikovsky's arguments and contained many inaccuracies, not surprisingly, because she had never read the book.

In referring to the events of the spring of 1950, Atwater had this to say:

> They suddenly decided to get rid of me ... All the evidence around me pointed to sheer cold panic. For example, I still retain the mental picture of one of the most composed, well-poised and

respected departmental heads, and scientist of some note as he came charging into my office unannounced, fire in his eyes, spitting in my face as he hurled abuse in a steady stream, then turning on his heel and slamming the door as he left. This came after I said I was letting the publisher use my name as author of the *This Week* article.

Atwater to Mrs. (Elisheva) Velikovsky

Gordon A. Atwater
324 Estchester Road
New Rochelle, New York 10801

July 4, 1982

Dear Elisheva,

The Shapley spell had been broken by the dire straights Hayden was in, financially, when I was put in there in full charge to try to save it and keep the doors open; something that I was successful in doing much to the amazement of the boards of trustees of both Hayden and the museum who said I had accomplished a miracle.

My appointment was not popular with astronomers; Shapley, in particular, who loved the adulation showered on him by the amateur astronomers who all considered Hayden to be their own territory. But my mission, at Hayden, was grim business because I had made it a vital part of the navy's officer and midshipman training programs, in WWII and it had to be kept viable for such possible use in the future.

In spite of Shapley's attitude toward me – which I knew all about – because Clyde Fisher thought I was going to drop him, when he came up for re-nomination, in 1947, and seemed to hurt about this, I finally decided to re-nominate him as a concession to Fisher even though I had no need whatsoever to consult with Shapley about anything. And it became increasingly clear that this only seemed to enrage him more.

Sincerely,

(Signed) Gordon

Other establishment scientists joined the collective campaign to suppress Velikovsky's book, all condemning "Worlds in Collision" in many book reviews that were syndicated and printed in newspapers that reached all corners of the country. The names changed: Harrison Brown, atomic scientist, Paul Herget, Director of the Observatory at the University of Cincinnati, Frank S. Hogg, Director of David Dunlop Observatory, University of Toronto. But, the reviews essentially remained the same. Payne-Gaposchkin's arguments were mimicked again and again complete with misquotes of Velikovsky's book. Ralph Juergens cites numerous examples of these misquotes in his article, »Minds in Chaos«; printed in *The Velikovsky Affair: Scientism vs. Science*, edited by Alfred de Grazia, Ralph E. Juergens and Livio C. Stecchini, University Books, New Hyde Park, New York, 1966.

Also *The Scientific American*, a highly respected journal, joined the "Scientific Watergate".

SCIENTIFIC AMERICAN
NEW YORK, NY

November 1, 1955

Mr. George Lovitt
Franklin Spier, Inc.
(advertising agency for Doubleday)

Dear George:

I write to you now to tell you that we are *turning down your order to publish your advertisement for Velikovsky's "Earth in Upheaval."*

Martin M. Davidson
Advertising Manager

SCIENTIFIC AMERICAN
NEW YORK, NY

September 4, 1956

Dear Dr. Velikovsky:

I think you should know my position once and for all. I think your books have done incalculable harm to the public understanding of what science is and what scientists do.

Dennis Flannagan
Editor

Waldemar Kaempffert, Science Editor of the New York Times, wrote to an assistant of Velikovsky, Adele Aronowitz, in a letter dated April 14, 1950:

Velikovsky's wild imaginings and so-called "proof" are without any scientific value whatever.

THE NEW YORK TIMES
TIMES SQUARE

January 5, 1950

Mr. Harry C. Stinnett
The Curtis Publishing Company
Independence Square
Philadelphia 5, PA

Dear Mr. Stinnett:

My thanks go to you for having sent me with your kind letter of December 23 Larrabee's article on Velikovsky's speculations entitled "Worlds in Collision."

It so happens that I read this opus weeks ago in galley proof. I almost wept to think that so much scholarship and time had been wasted on a supposition of which the astronomers and mathematicians are sure to make mincemeat. It is enough to say here that not an animal or a plant would have remained alive if a comet of the huge mass assumed by Velikovsky ever approached within a million miles of the earth. In other words there would have been no written records for Velikovsky to study and interpret.

Sincerely yours,

(Signed) Waldemar Kaempffert
Science Editor

UNIVERSITY OF ARIZONA
TUCSON
STEWARD OBSERVATORY

May 29, 1952

Professor Robert N. Pfeiffer
Department of Semitic Language
And History
Harvard University
Cambridge 38, Massachusetts

Dear Professor Pfeiffer:

In the May number of Harper's magazine, on page 107, is an advertisement of the Doubleday Company for Velikovsky's new book, "Ages in Chaos." This advertisement quotes you as follows regarding the author's claims in his book:

"His conclusions are amazing, unheard of, revolutionary, sensational. If his findings are accepted by historians, all present histories for the period before Alexander the Great must be discarded, and completely rewritten. If Dr. Velikovsky is right, this volume is the greatest contribution to the investigation of ancient times ever written."

I invite your attention particularly to the statement at the top of the advertisement to the effect that the book "Worlds in Collision" rocked the scientific world. It did not rock any scientific world. It was never even advertised, by either of its publishers, Macmillan or Doubleday, in any scientific journal or magazine that I have been able to find in our University Library. On the contrary, the sales promotion was conducted only in publications usually accessible to the scientifically uninformed. The only world that was rocked was the publishing world, because of the ethical nadir to which it descended.

(Signed) Edwin F. Carpenter
Director, Steward Observatory

14 years after the publication of Worlds in Collision

MEMO from the desk of JOYCE WILLIG
HARRY WALKER, INC.

May 4, 1964

TO: Dr. Harlow Shapley

Dear Dr. Shapley:

Professor Robert Gallo of Auburn Community College, Auburn, New York, is interested in having you appear on a lecture program there with Immanuel Velikovsky.

Would you consider appearing on a program with Dr. Velikovsky? Please let me hear from you on this as soon as possible.

My best to Mrs. Shapley. Warmest regards.

Cordially,

(Signed) Joyce Willig
Sales Representative

To Joyce Willig from Harlow Shapley
(Handwritten on The Benjamin Franklin Hotel stationary)

Oh, no! No! Oh, no! Don't get trapped! He is a dangerous crank.

(Signed) H. S.

MEMO from the desk of JOYCE WILLIG
HARRY WALKER, INC.

May 11, 1964

Mr. Robert Gallo
Convocation Chairman
Auburn Community College
Auburn, New York

Dear Mr. Gallo:

What are you trying to do to me! Enclosed please find my answer from Dr. Shapley. On my lunch hour, my first stop will be the library to find out more about Immanuel Velikovsky.

Are you interested in an appearance by Dr. Shapley *alone*? Please let me hear from you.

Cordially,

(Signed) Joyce Willig
Sales Representative

Shapley to Professor Burgstahler

July 2, 1967

Dear Professor Burgstahler:

As you probably suspect I find little happiness in reading or thinking about Velikovsky. He seems to be one of our most erudite charlatans.

He may lead his life as he sees fit; but I am somewhat ashamed of the Y.S.M

(Signed) Harlow Shapley

Burgstahler to Walter Sullivan

DEPARTMENT OF CHEMISTRY
THE UNIVERSITY OF KANSAS
LAWRENCE, KANSAS

August 19, 1969

Mr. Walter Sullivan
Science Editor
The New York Times
Times Square
New York, N.Y.

Dear Mr. Sullivan:

In view of the report of the presence of larger-than-expected amounts of neon and argon in the lunar samples brought back by the Apollo II crew, I thought you might like to see this copy

cont'd

Burgstahler to Walter Sullivan (cont'd)

of a letter Dr. Immanuel Velikovsky wrote to me on Wednesday, July 23, 1969, before the mission had returned. On page 2 he suggests the presence of argon and neon from the 8th century B.C. encounter he believes Mars had with the moon. (In his book Worlds in Collision he already proposed the presence of these gases in significant amounts on Mars.)

For the "record" then, it should be noted that Dr. Velikovsky anticipated the presence of neon and argon entrapped in lunar rocks. The origin of these gases in these rocks is of course open to other interpretations, but at least the explanation he offers is not unreasonable if his historical account is correct. With the high frequency of lunar "quakes" being recorded by the seismometer, his suggestion of a molten or partially molten lunar surface as recently as the 8th century B.C. takes on added interest.

With best wishes.

Sincerely yours,

(Signed) Alber W. Burgstahler
Professor of Chemistry

Cc: Dr. Velikovsky

To Shapley from a high school student (letter sent in March 1969)

Dear Sir:

I am a high school student preparing a research paper, which is a prerequisite for graduation. My subject is the controversy surrounding some of Dr. Emmanuel Velikovsky's theories presented in his book, Worlds in Collision.

Have the relatively recent geological and oceanographic discoveries concerning the massive deposits of cosmic debris, the evidence of a shift in the earth's polarity, and the discoveries of Mariner II affected your opinion in any way?

H.S. (initials signed)

Shapley's response to the student

HARVARD COLLEGE OBSERVATORY
CAMBRIDGE, MASS

March 8, 1969

All professional astronomers consider Velikovsky a fraud. Can't you find a reputable subject [for] your research paper?

(Signed) Harlow Shapley

GORDON A. ATWATER
324 Eastchester Road
New Rochelle, New York

January 2, 1964

Mr. John Fischer, Editor in Chief
Harper's Magazine
49 East 33rd Street
New York, NY

Dear Mr. Fischer:

I commend Harper's for reopening the Velikovsky debate. This is long since overdue. Had Velikovsky received a respectful hearing in 1950, all questions could have been convincingly disposed of there and then. However, he did not receive such a hearing; instead he was made to suffer the deep humiliation of being completely discredited, subjected to censorship and condemnation and was shunted out of education by top men and institutions. As has been pointed out, scientists who were ignorant of what Velikovsky has done were the ones who discredited him with extreme ruthlessness. Even today, Larrabee shows us he has one idea of what Velikovsky – perhaps more nearly correct – has done. Bailey shows he has somewhat different ideas, and Menzel shows us in his "Rejoinder" a completely different idea. I think it is at least reasonable to ask that before we subject a man to these grave indignities and completely discredit him we all make a reasonable effort to understand what he has been saying. There is evidence no such effort was made in 1959 and we see no effort being made today and we are indebted to Harper's for showing us that such a frightful condition has continued to exist ever since 1950, during years when all mankind is crying for a solution to the grave space-age problems which have come to us these past seven years since Sputnik I. I call this very responsible journalism in the highest tradition of what America stands for.

I planned to feature Velikovsky's work in a special show where each branch of science as well as the public generally would be able to quickly grasp what he had done and how each science and discipline was involved. We would have been tapping the crystal clear water of the spring from which flow our most vital, important and constructive human resources.

The same hysterical pressures which Larrabee says forced Macmillan to drop the book caused this show to be cancelled – even after I announced we would have it, and forced me out of science and education.

For five years, we had been perfecting new ways to establish a strong channel of communication between sciences. The Velikovsky show "Worlds in Collision" was to be the acid test which would prove the soundness of this new medium of cultural expression embracing the arts, sciences, drama, music and literature. Had we been successful, we would have reached a new and higher level – badly needed – of cultural attainment. We would have been promoting better planning for the space age, which was just beyond our horizon then and seven years ahead. It is possible we might have helped speed up investigations of space and accelerated the space program. I will leave it to others to estimate what percentage of the billions of dollars we have been committing ourselves to in research and development in the space program would have been more wisely spent, or actually saved, had Velikovsky received a respectful hearing in the Hayden Planetarium and the American Museum of Natural History, Harvard University, etc., etc.

It is ironic that Velikovsky's theories were not allowed to reach the testing platform – seven years before Sputnik I left the launching pad, ushering in the space age and making it necessary for Bargmann and Motz in their famous letter to Science to call attention to Velikovsky's right to priority of prediction in the three instances they mention. We agreed in 1946 that if these three theories were proved this would provide powerful support for Velikovsky's methods and hypotheses. These theo-

cont'd

Atwater to Harper's (cont'd)

ries were and still are a powerful integrating force and could have been the instrument which showed the way to the most effective method of communicating between the sciences and thus bringing all branches into a harmonious and effective force for the good of men everywhere.

I have been silent about Velikovsky since I wrote the cover story for This Week magazine (April 2, 1950) at their request, just before the appearance of which I had been banished from science and education: the two fields to which I had been drafted by the U.S. Navy in 1942 and then, in 1945, asked by the American Museum of Natural History and the Hayden Planetarium to dedicate the rest of my life to this work for the good of the country, in preference to continuing in the Navy as many had been urging me to do.

Cordially yours,

(Signed) Gordon A. Atwater
Until 1950, Chairman & Curator,
The Hayden Planetarium and
The American Museum of Natural History

E. R. Langenbach to Harvard Crimson

August 16, 1976

The Editor
Harvard Crimson

Dear Sir:

I am writing to you on the assumption that The Crimson has not lost interest in using its influence to see that grievous wrongs are righted, particularly when a section of the academic community of Harvard University was involved in perpetrating the wrongs. I refer to the grossly unjust treatment accorded to a great scholar, Immanuel Velikovsky, by the scientific establishment, particularly by the astronomers, and more particularly by members of the staff of The Harvard Crimson.

Dr. Velikovsky is now 81 years old. If anything is to be done to make amends for the mistreatment he has suffered. it is obvious that it should be done now, or as soon as possible.

I have only discovered one member of the Harvard faculty who treated Velikovsky with respect, understanding and sympathy, although it is possible that there were others. He was the late Dr. Robert H. Pfeiffer.

In 1963, Princeton scientist, Harry H. Hess, who was then chairman of the Space Science Board of The National Academy of Sciences, wrote in a letter to Velikovsky:

> You have after all predicted that Jupiter would be a source of radio noise, that Venus would have a high surface temperature, that the Sun and bodies of the solar system would have large electrical charges and several other such predictions. Some of the predictions were said to be impossible when you made them. All of them were predicted long before proof that they were correct came to hand.

cont'd

E. R. Langenbach to Harvard Crimson (cont'd)

Before closing, I would like to ask a few pertinent questions. If Velikovsky were a "crackpot", "charlatan", or "fraud", would any of the following events have occurred?

Would Albert Einstein have taken the time to read Velikovsky's books and manuscripts and to spend any hours discussing his theories with him?

Would the late Professor Harry Hammond Hess, former Chairman of Princeton's geology department and subsequently chairman of the Space Science Board of the National Academy of Sciences *have given Velikovsky several opportunities to address the faculty and graduate students in his department at Princeton?*

Would Professor Lloyd Motz, Columbia University astronomer, and Professor V. Bargmann, physicist, of Princeton, have joined in writing a letter to Science, which was published in the issue of December 21, 1962, pointing out the recent confirmations of Velikovsky's claims, and urging that Velikovsky's other conclusions should be re-examined without prejudice? And would Professor Motz have stated also (Harper's, October 1963) that Velikovsky's ideas "should be considered by responsible scholars and scientists as the creation of a serious and dedicated investigator ... His writings should be carefully studied because they're the product of an extraordinary and brilliant mind, and are based upon some of the most concentrated and penetrating scholarship of our period ..."?

Would Professor Van Houten of Princeton have made Earth in Upheaval required reading in his course on paleontology shortly after its publication in 1955.

Would Robert Pfeiffer, Orientalist and biblical scholar, and Walter S. Adams, astronomer, of Mt. Wilson Observatory have extended their assistance and support to him, as they did?

Would Velikovsky have been able successfully to predict that radio noises would be heard emanating from Jupiter, contrary to Einstein's belief?

Would Velikovsky have been able correctly to predict, contrary to accepted beliefs, that Venus was extremely hot; that its atmosphere was very heavy; that the earth had a magneto-sphere beyond the ionosphere; that the magnetosphere extended as far as the lunar orbit; that Jupiter was a source of radio signals; that remnant magnetism would he discovered in the lunar rocks; that petroleum hydrocarbons can be converted to edible substances; that the sun, moon, many of the planets and interstellar space are electrically charged and not just affected by gravitation and light pressure, etc., etc., etc.?

Would Velikovsky have been repeatedly and insistently have sought scientific tests of his conclusions? (Don't charlatans and frauds *avoid* tests?)

Finally, would the astronomers, physicists and other scientists and scholars across the country who attacked Velikovsky, who called him names instead of reading his books, and answering them (if they could), who substituted scorn and vituperation for logical discourse, who, when Velikovsky's claims were eventually proved, one after another, still repeatedly tried, by the device of ex post facto "ad hoc theorizing", to discredit him? Nevertheless, would they have taken these extraordinary measures if they had really thought that he was a "charlatan" or "intellectual fraud"? I do not believe so. Wasn't it possibly that they, or at least many of them, realized, with dismay, that he was right and that what they had been writing, preaching and teaching had been inaccurate all along? Wasn't it that they felt they had to discredit him – but should not debate him seriously, point by point, on the issues? And wasn't part of it resentment, perhaps, against an outsider who was not an astronomer, physicist, geologist or archeologist – who did not even have a telescope – but who dared to step in and destroy many of the sacred dogmas or each of those disciplines, irrevocably? I think so. I believe they could probably have discredited a fraud or charlatan within a few months, but *they haven't succeeded in discrediting Velikovsky in thirty years!*

Please let me know, after you have completed your investigation, whether you agree that *Harvard at least owes Velikovsky recognition, even at this late date, for his outstanding scholarship, high intellectual integrity, extraordinary logic, vision*

cont'd

E. R. Langenbach to Harvard Crimson (cont'd)

> *and tolerance, and for post-space-age thinking long before there was a space-age.* Many honorary degrees have been granted to persons who deserved them less, and, I suggest, few have been awarded to more deserving intellectuals. Why would such recognition not be appropriate in the case of Dr. Immanuel Velikovsky?
>
> Sincerely,
>
> (Signed) E. R. Langenbach

On November 28, 1977, *The Harvard Crimson* ran an article written by Steven A. Wasserman, entitled *Some Should Not Be Heard*, and about Velikovsky stated:

> An educated public would not buy Velikovsky any more than they would protein hair conditioners, timed release aspirin, Geritol, or other such fakes. Until then, their ignorance will most likely bring scientists into many more close encounters of the Velikovsky kind.

THE NEW YORK TIMES
TIMES SQUARE
NEW YORK, N.Y. 10036

July 2, 1969

Dear Dr. Velikovsky:

The New York Times is preparing a special supplement for which it would welcome some comment from you on the moon landing. The supplement will be out before the event and the deadline for this is July 14. We have asked for responses ranging between 200 and 400 words from such men as André Malraux, Reinhold Niebuhr, Peter Kapitza, Isaiha Berlin and C.P. Snow.

The two key questions are: What does the moon landing mean to mankind – historically, scientifically, philosophically and culturally? What does it mean to you personally?

I would be most grateful if you could consider this request apart from any similar commitments you may have made to other publications. I would gladly come out to Princeton or, if you preferred, you might write me if you decide, hopefully, to give us your views.

I remain,

Yours faithfully,

(Signed) Henry Raymont

Dr. Immanuel Velikovsky's article entitled *Are Moon's Scars Only 3,000 Years Old?* appeared on the front page of the early edition of the July 21, 1969 *The New York Times.* By the afternoon/late edition of the *Times,* the article had been replaced by an article entitled *Technology a Spur to Changes in Religion,* by Edward B. Fiske.

The following is the article *Are Moon's Scars Only 3,000 Years Old?* as it appeared in the July 21, 1969 *The New York Times.*

Dr. Velikovsky is the author of "Worlds in Collision" and several other books arguing that cataclysmic astronomical events have helped shape human history. His books, despite their popularity, have evoked strong reactions from the scientific community.

Are Moon's Scars Only 3,000 Years Old?
By Immanuel Velikovsky

Man, free from the bonds tying him to the rock of his birth, is about to make his first steps on the lunar landscape. It is an amazing achievement of man's technological genius and with it the first stage of the Space Age (1957-1969) will be concluded.

These 12 years have been unkind to many accredited scientific theories of the solar system. Some of the most fundamental concepts are being summoned for revision.

In celestial mechanics, all new evidence has conjured against the concept – basic in science until very recently – that gravitation and inertia are the only forces in action in the celestial sphere.

The new discoveries are the interplanetary magnetic field centered on the sun and rotating with it; the solar plasma; the terrestrial magnetosphere that caused the moon to rock when entering and leaving the magnetic funnel; the enormously powerful magnetic envelope around Jupiter through which the Galilean satellites plow, themselves influencing the Jovian radio signals.

Who is the physicist that would insist that Jupiter, traveling with its powerful magnetosphere through the interplanetary magnetic field, is not affected by it? Or that the Jovian satellites are not influenced in their motions by the magnetic field of their primary?

And in cosmology the puzzling discoveries have been Venus's incandescent heat; its massive atmosphere (140 atmospheric pressures!); its retrograde rotation controlled by the earth (it turns the very same face to us when in inferior conjunctions), and its mountain-high ground tides (this is my understanding of the paradoxical altitude readings of the recent Venera 5 and 6), which also have caused it in the past to acquire a nearly circular orbit; Mars's moon-like surface and its apparent loss of a large part of its rotational momentum (Mariner 4), and the moon's active state – it is not a dead body cold to its core.

Establishing the Timing

All these discoveries unite to defend the thesis that the present order of the solar system is of recent date.

In divergence from accepted views, I maintain that less than 3,000 years ago the moon's surface was repeatedly molten and its surface bubbled. Since the nineteen-fifties, many unburst bubbles – domes – have been observed on the moon and gases have been found escaping from several orifices.

The moon has hundreds of hot spots and even its light is not all reflected solar light; researchers have come up with calculations that fluorescence would not account for the rest.

In thermoluminescence tests, it should be possible to establish the recentness of the last heating (melting!) of the lunar surface. For that purpose, astronauts need to take samples from about three feet below the surface, to where the long lunar day hardly transmits any solar heat. Such tests could establish the time when the lunar surface was molten.

The moon has a very weak magnetic field; yet its rocks and lavas could conceivably be rich in remnant magnetism resulting from strong currents when in the embrace of exogenous magnetic fields.

Before their removal from the ground, the specimens should be marked as to their orientation in situ. Meteorites could not fall all similarly aligned. This simple performance of marking the orientation of samples, I was told, is not in the program of the first landing.

Despite the fact that there are no oceans on the moon and no marine life to give origin to petroleum hydrocarbons, I would not be surprised if bitumens, (asphalt, tar or waxes) or carbides or carbonates are found in the composition of the rocks, although not necessarily in the first few samples.

Deposits of Petroleum

A visitor to the earth would not detect deposits of petroleum in the first few hours, either. I have claimed an extraterrestrial origin for some of the deposits of petroleum on earth; the moon did not escape the same shower. Only in a subsequent melting of the ground, such deposits would most probably convert into carbides or carbonates.

It is quite probable that chlorine, sulphur and iron in various compounds, possibly (the Deluge) and subsequently was covered for several centuries by water, which dissociated under the ultra-violet rays of the sun, with hydrogen escaping into space.

I maintain that – although not already at the first landing – an excessively strong radioactivity will be detected in localized areas, in those among the crater formations that resulted, I contend, from interplanetary discharges.

I also maintain that moonquakes must be so numerous that there is a bit of a chance that during their few hours on the moon the astronauts may experience a quake.

Some authorities (Harold Urey among them) claim that the scars on the face of the moon are older than four and a half billion years. The lunar landings will provide the answer: Was the face of the moon as we see it carved over four and a half billion years ago or, as I believe, less than 3,000 years ago.

If this unorthodox view is substantiated, it will bear greatly not only on many fields of science but also on the phenomenon of repression of racial memories, with all the implications as to man's irrational behavior.

DOUBLEDAY
A COMMUNICATIONS CORPORATION

March 20, 1978

Dr. Immanuel Velikovsky
78 Hartley Avenue
Princeton, New Jersey 08540

Dear Dr. Velikovsky:

Brad has been giving me reports on you regularly and I do want to say that I hope you are not too disheartened by the unfair and prejudiced attacks on you in connection with the Cornell publication. Brad said how badly they treated you, giving Sagan all the time in the world to revise and amend his remarks and correct his mistakes and giving you next to no time at all. I think this sort of thing should be documented so that we can one day work it into an account of the continuing or intermittent campaigns against Velikovsky.

But these attacks are weakened by their cheapness and over the long turn of history, and very likely even in the short run, they will be seen for what they are.

Meanwhile, Brad has some excellent ideas for the further of your works, including the contract, etc. and I know that he is working on them steadily.

Be of good cheer. The opinion of the world does not rest on a Cornell publication nor does the world turn on the opinions of Carl C. Sagan and a few others.

Best,

(Signed) Samuel Vaughan
Publisher

Cc: Mr. Walter Bradbury

Velikovsky's Predictions in 1950

Ancient History

1. **Velikovsky said the Bronze Age ended in a catastrophe. Establishment science and historians said no such evidence exists.** Claude F. A. Schaeffer concluded from his analysis of the archaeological digs across the Middle East that a great upheaval (not caused by the actions of man) destroyed all civilizations in the Bronze Age.

2. **Velikovsky said after the Bronze Age ended the climate of the Earth changed radically. Historians claimed man destroyed the environment.** Velikovsky's view was presented by a Yale University professor in the Sciences, (May-June 1996) and is being supported by new research.

3. **Velikovsky said ancient history was shorter by about 500 years. Establishment historians claimed there was no possibility of a shortening of such length.** Digs carried out in Syria proved history was shorter for Mesopotamian history. See Gunnar Heinsohn: »Who were the Hyksos?« *VI Congresso Internazionale di Egittologia* Vol. 2 (Torino Italy 1993).

4. **Velikovsky said that Ancient Egyptian history is not based on solid foundations and therefore must be in error. Establishment historians said there is little room available to move any dynasty either back or forward in time.** Professor Lynn E. Rose using the El Lahun papyrus has proved that the 12th dynasty of Egypt dated to the second millennium B.C. (based on astronomical data of the Moon and Sirius in this papyrus) must be placed over 1460 years closer to the present. See Lynn E. Rose: »From Calendars to Chronology«" in *Stephen J. Gould and Immanuel Velikovsky* (Dale Ann Pearlman ed.) (Forest Hills NY, 1996).

5. **Velikovsky claimed that Minoan B script writings unearthed on Crete and in the Peloponnesus are Greek. Fifty of the world's most noted Hellenistic scholars previously canvassed were unanimous that they did not expect the script to be Greek nor did the translator Michael Ventris believe this would be the case.** But, Ventris proved this script to be an ancient form of the Greek language. See J. Chadwick: *The Decipherment of Linear B*, (NY 1958) esp. pp. 67-100.

6. **Velikovsky claimed Mesoamerican culture is several centuries older than the date assigned to it in traditional historical chronology. George Kubler wrote, "The Mesoamerican cosmology to which Velikovsky repeatedly appeals for proof did not originate until the beginning of our era." (*American Journal of Science*, vol. 248, 1950).** Ralph E. Juergens, however, reported in the December 1956 issue of *National Geographic Society*, "Atomic science has proved that ancient civilization of Mexico to be some 1000 years older than had been believed!" See Ralph E. Juergens: »Minds in Chaos« in *The Velikovsky Affair*, (de Grazia, ed.), p. 28, and P. Drucker, et al.: »Radiocarbon Dates from La Venta, Tabasco« *Science*, vol. 126, July 1957, pp. 72-73, and Richard S. MacNeish: »The Origins of New World Civilization«, *Scientific American*, vol. 221, November 1964, pp. 29-37.

7. **Velikovsky claimed the long day of Joshua in the Middle East coincided with the long night in the Americas as reported in ancient traditional literature. Critics to this day say "The problem for Velikovsky is that he has no time control on the ... [American] reference; it just happened in the remote past.** This should have caused him to stand back from the evidence and define a defensible approach. Only if some very specific information linked the independent references could they be used in support." As reported by Mike Baillie: *Exodus to Arthur*, London 1949, p. 173, Z. Sitchin citing the historical work of Fernando Montesinos: *Memorias Antiguas Historiales de Peru* (1600s) translated for the Haley Society in London in 1920, proved that the year of the Long Day of Joshua was the same year as the Long Night in the Americas. See Z. Sitchin: *The Lost Realms*, New York 1990, pp. 151-154.

Electromagnetism and the Sun

8. **Velikovsky claimed that space is not a vacuum and that electromagnetism plays a fundamental role in our solar system and the entire universe.** This thesis is no longer controversial since the discovery of Jupiter's radio noises and the Earth's magnetosphere (the Van Allen Belts) and the interplanetary magnetic field found respectively in 1955, 1958 and 1960.

9. **Velikovsky claimed the Sun is an electrically charged body. On October 15, 1952, in the *Proceeding of the American Philosophical Society*, D. Menzel, a Harvard astronomer, purported to show that the Sun can not hold a charge above 1800 volts, if positive (and only a single volt, if negative).** He asserted that Velikovsky's mode requires a charge of 10 to the 19th power (10^{19}) volts. Eight years later, Professor V.A. Bailey of the University of Sidney, Australia, unaware of this debate, concluded that the Sun carries a net negative charge on the order of 10^{19} volts (!) in »Existence of Net Electric Charge on Stars«, *Nature*, vol. 186, May 14, 1960, p. 508, and in *Nature*, vol. 189, January 7 and March 25, 1961, pp. 43-45 and 994-995. It was discovered in 1960 that the newly discovered interplanetary magnetic field is centered on the Sun and rotates with it.

10. **Velikovsky claimed that magnetic binary stars in orbit around each other are not moving in a purely gravitational environment and that electromagnetism plays a role in the behavior of such stars. James Warwick, using standard equations, came to the conclusion that observable phenomena of such stars do not derive from these equations.** What was found is that there are "observable phenomena" related to these magnetic stars but not to similar stars without measurable magnetic fields. The magnetic stars rotate quite slowly as opposed to those without intrinsic magnetic fields, and those with strong magnetic fields are almost all single or if they have companions these are extremely distant. Magnetic stars with tiny fields (Am stars) are all extremely close to their companion. M. Floquet in »Les Etoiles Ap [magnetic star] Binaires«, in *Astronomy and Astrophysics Abstracts*, vol. 30, Part 1, 1983, p.434, claimed:

"The magnetic fields seem to play an important role in the relation between binarity and the Ap phenomenon." Warwick has never responded to this evidence.

11. **Velikovsky claimed electromagnetism in the universe can affect the motions of the celestial bodies. Equations of astrophysics were said to deny any such phenomenon.** Vera Rubin, of the Carnegie Institute in Washington, D.C., discovered that stars in spiral galaxies do not obey Kepler and Newton or Einstein's equations of celestial motion. Unlike the planets which travel more slowly as their orbits are situated more distant from the Sun, stars at a certain distance from the center of their galaxies all travel at about the same speed no matter how far beyond that point they are located. Eduardo Battaner, of the Department of Theoretical Physics and Cosmology at the University of Granada, Spain, in the journal *Astronomy*, Winter 1993-1994, pp. 50-54, explained these errant stellar motions in terms of magnetism.

12. **Velikovsky claimed that the solar system had been unstable in the past and that planets had changed their orbits. This was the major objection to his theory by the scientific establishment.** In »Doing the Poincaré Shuffle«, *Scientific American*, January 1997, pp. 116 and 118, astronomer Philip Morrison wrote that the solar system was not stable, that planets can change orbits, be captured by the Sun or even thrown out of the solar system. Although the time element is not short enough to support Velikovsky, solar system stability is no longer an obstacle to his thesis. A test in space has been devised to determine the question of electromagnetism's role in celestial motion. See Charles Ginenthal: *The Electro-Gravitic Theory of Celestial Motion and Cosmology*, Forest Hills, NY 1999, pp. 134-154.

Venus

13. **Velikovsky claimed Venus was a new planet in the early cool-down period of its birth. The scientists had several versions and visions of Venus, but none suggested Venus would be a volcanic cauldron.** See Lawrence Colin: »Basic Facts About Venus«, *Venus* (D.M. Hunten, et al, eds.), Tucson, AZ 1983, p. 13. Magellan spacecraft mapped and made radar measurements that showed "The entire planet is one big volcano." [Henry S.F. Cooper, Jr.: *The Evening Star*, New York 1993, p. 180] Richard Kerr, editor of *Science* claimed that when planetary geologists "look at the surface [of Venus] itself, they see a newborn babe." See R. A. Kerr: »Venus is looking too Pristine«, *Science*, vol. 250, November 16, 1990, p. 912.

14. **Velikovsky claimed that the great heat emitted from Venus came from the hot planet. Planetary scientists and astronomers claimed Venus is heated by a "Runaway Greenhouse Effect."** See Carl Sagan: »Problem VIII. The Temperature of Venus«, *Scientists Confront Velikovsky* (D. Goldsmith, ed.), Cornell 1977, pp.78-83. However, as presented in *Venus* (ed. by Hunten cited above, p. 657-658) all the Pioneer spacecraft's measurements above the Venusian cloud tops showed the planet was giving off more heat than the Runaway Greenhouse permitted. Richard A. Kerr, reporting on the middle atmosphere, said of the Pioneer, Venus probes: "each one found more energy being radiated up from the lower atmosphere then enter it as sunlight [and] the size of the apparent upward flow of energy varies from place to place by a factor of 2, which is a disturbing discovery." See R. A. Kerr: »Venus Not Simple or Familiar, but Interesting«, *Science,* vol. 207, 1980, p. 289. A. Seiff claimed that the Venera 910, 11 and 12 probes to the surface of Venus found 40 times on average more heat coming from the planet than the Runaway Greenhouse will allow. See A. Seiff: »Thermal Structure of the Atmosphere of Venus«, *Venus* (Hunten, et al, eds.), Tucson, AZ, 1983, p. 226. All sets of spacecraft measurements at face value indicate Venus is the source of nearly all its great heat.

15. **Velikovsky claimed that the clouds of Venus would be composed of hydrocarbons. The scientific establishment denied this possibility, see Carl Sagan:** »Problem VII The Clouds of Venus«, *Scientists Confront Velikovsky*, Cornell 1977, pp. 73-78. Thomas H. Donahue in *Science News*, September 12, 1992, p. 172 admitted there was sharp spike in the amount of methane in Venus' atmosphere.

16. **Velikovsky claimed that the close interactions between Venus and the Earth may have caused it to rotate in the opposite direction of the other planets. This prediction ran against everything believed to explain the formation of planets.** When the retrograde rotation of Venus was confirmed, it was discovered that at their closest alignment with the Sun, Venus almost precisely shows the same hemisphere to the Earth, which would be expected from a very close approach. If Venus had a mass anomaly it would develop this relationship with the sun which is gravitationally more influential than the Earth on Venus. Hoimar Von Ditfurth in *Children of the Universe*, New York 1976, p.115, came to the conclusion that "the Earth must once have exerted a braking or decelerating effect on Venus until the two planets' mutual gravitational attraction brought about the 'coupling' we see today."

17. **Velikovsky claimed Venus would have oxygen in its atmosphere. This was discovered. To get around this evidence Sagan claimed there was a "dearth of O_2 on Venus."** See Carl Sagan: »Some Other Problems«, *Scientists Confront Velikovsky* (D. Goldsmith ed.), Cornell 1977, p. 87. But Venus' atmosphere is about 90 times the mass of that of the Earth's and a finding of say one percent of oxygen would be equal to about 90 percent of the Earth's atmosphere. The finding of a fraction of one percent still proves Venus contains a great deal of oxygen as Velikovsky claimed.

Moon

18. **Velikovsky claimed the moon had been subjected to great tidal distortions from near approaches of Venus, and these interactions created a high thermal gradient in the moon.** See *The New York Times*, July 21, 1964 (early city edition). On the other hand, **"The professional astronomers had solidly maintained for decades that the moon was completely dead, cold right through …"** See Dundan Lunan: *New Worlds for Old*, New York 1979, p. 79. When the high thermal gradient was discovered, some scientists "suggested … instrument malfunctions." See *Time* magazine, January 24, 1972, p. 67

19. **Velikovsky claimed that these great recent tidal disruptions would leave the Moon with discontinuities beneath its surface that would still be adjusting to the pressures and therefore there would be numerous moonquakes. Lunan (cited above) claimed professional astronomers said that the Moon was "a world without activity apart from the occasional meteor strike."** Nevertheless, seismic instruments left on the Moon showed that it was experiencing deep (600 to 800 kilometers) quakes below the surface and nearly all were located on the side of the Moon. (See French: *The Moon Book*, New York 1977, p. 228) At these depths, rock does not suddenly move. (Cliff Frolich: »Deep Earthquakes«, *Scientific American*, vol. 260, January 1989, p. 48) The pressures above cause rock to flow slowly. G. Latham et al., admitted these deep moonquakes were "releasing strains of unknown origin." (See G. Latham, et al.: *Science*, vol. 174, 1971, pp. 687-692)

20. **Velikovsky claimed the majority of lunar craters resulted from the collapse of large bubbles which occurred during Venus' near approaches that heated the Moon. The present paradigm is that nearly all lunar craters are of impact origin.** Nevertheless, hundreds of domes that are in the form of rising bubbles have been found on the Moon with circular craters directly on the top of these domes. See *Science* (January 13, 1970), which reported this finding. Impacts would not strike hundreds of domes at their central apex.

21. **Velikovsky claimed evidence of petroleum hydrocarbons will be found on the Moon. This ran counter to the theory that hydrocarbons are produced by life forms.** Yet, evidence of organic matter (aromatic hydrocarbons) was found in several samples of lunar material returned by the Apollo XI mission. See C. Pollamparuma, et al.: »Search for Organic Compounds in Lunar Samples: Pyrolysis Products, Hydrocarbons, Amino Acids«, *Science*, vol. 167, January 30, 1970, pp. 760-762; and P. I. Abell, et al.: »Ingenous Lunar Methane and Ethane«, *Nature*, vol. 226, April 18, 1970, pp. 251-252.

22. **Velikovsky claimed hydrocarbons left on the lunar surface must have been converted to carbides.** Carbide rocks were found on the lunar surface. See G. Eglington, et al.: *Nature*, vol. 226, April 18, 1970, pp. 251-252.

23. **Velikovsky claimed that lunar rocks will reveal remnant magnetism caused by interplanetary electrical discharges, despite the fact that the Moon itself has an exceedingly weak magnetic field. This was not in any way expected by the lunar scientists.** Yet, one of the most puzzling finds of Apollo XI is the magnetic remnance in lunar rocks. See D. W. Strangway, et al.: »Magnetic Properties of Lunar Samples«, along with R. R. Doell, et at.: »Magnetic Studies of Lunar Samples« and S. K. Runcorn, et al.: »Magnetic Properties of Lunar Samples«, *Science*, vol. 167, January 1970, pp. 691-693, 695-697 and 697-699. As late as 1999, James A. Van Allen admitted that finding the solution to how the "Moon could have developed such magnetized patches remain a nagging problem." See James A. Van Allen and Frances Gagenal: »Planetary Magnetospheres and the Interplanetary Medium«, *The New Solar System*, 4th edition (J. Kelly Beatty, et al., eds.), Cambridge, MA 1999, p. 54. After almost fifty years, the researchers cannot find a solution to this phenomenon.

24. **Velikovsky claimed that lunar rocks will be found to contain excessive inclusions of argon and neon from an extraneous source; on the basis of potassium-argon dating the age of the Moon will be calculated as older than the solar system itself.** Very rich inclusions of argon and neon were found in lunar rocks. Based on potassium-argon dating some of

the rocks gave an unacceptable age of seven billion years. At least two Apollo XII rocks have been dated at 20 billion years. See *Philadelphia Evening Bulletin*, January 6, 1970, and Whitcome and Dc Young: *Science*, vol. 167, 1970.

25. **Velikovsky claimed interplanetary electrical discharges would also generate localized spots of excessively strong radioactivity on the lunar surface.** According to Allen L. Hammond: »Lunar Research: No Agreement on Evolutionary Models«, *Science*, vol. 175, 1972, pp. 868-870, the finding of higher radioactivity elements on the Moon's surface, as they appear to be, has been difficult for geochemists to explain.

26. **Velikovsky claimed that thermoluminescence of lunar core will show a thermal process in historical times. The report by R. Walker of Washington University, St. Louis, sent to NASA on TL tests on shallow cores (about six inches deep) refers to thermal activity about 10,000 years ago. Velikovsky suggested in a letter dated July 23, 1969 to *The New York Times* that the cores should be taken from a depth of three feet, where the solar heat of the long lunar day does not penetrate.** See Charles Ginenthal: »The Moon in Upheaval«, *The Velikovskian*, vol. 1, No. 1, 1993, pp. 89-92, and »Oberg's Unscientific Method«, *The Velikovskian*, vol. 1 , No. 2, 1993, pp. 66-70.

Mars

27. **Velikovsky claimed that Mars' interactions with Venus would leave it as a "dead planet ... with rifts and cracks" that show immense tidal stresses were placed on that body. The scientific establishment's view expressed by Professor Robert Leighton of the California Institute of Technology claimed that "There are no mountain ranges, no great faults, no extensive volcanic fields, in fact, no evidence of volcanic activity."** (Kenneth F. Weaver: »Voyage to the Planets«, *National Geographic*, August 1970, pp. 169-173.) Carl Sagan's

»Mars. A New World To Explore«, *National Geographic*, December 1967, p. 828, claimed that Mars would exhibit "a gently sloping landscape." Patrick Moore: *The New Guide to the Moon*, New York 1976, p. 193, states "The Martian scene proved to be utterly unlike what most people had expected. Instead of gentle, rolling plains, there were mountains, valleys, craters and volcanoes." The utter devastation of the Martian terrain drove a geologist Bill Beatty to suggest "a Velikovskian-type scenario such as a passing close encounter event" occurred to Mars. See Randolph R. Pozos: *The Face of Mars*, Chicago 1986, p. 60. Michael Carr, an expert of Mars, on page 69 of the same book "believes a sudden disaster occurred on Mars."

28. **Velikovsky claimed Mars must have changed its orbit from one closer to the Sun to that which it follows today. Astronomers rejected this based on their view of solar system stability.** However, hundreds of thousands of river valley systems with dendritic feeder streams have been found on Mars. (D. Wallace and Carl Sagan: »Evaporation of Ice in Interplanetary Atmospheres: Ice-covered Rivers on Mars«, *Icarus*, vol. 39, 1979, pp. 385-400. The problem is that Mars has always been too far from the Sun to allow water to flow on its surface and all research into creating sufficient heat through its atmosphere have failed. (Charles Ginenthal: »The Oceans and Rivers of Mars«, *Proceedings of the Immanuel Velikovsky Centennial Celebration, 1895-1995*, Forest Hills, New York, 1996, pp. 132-168.)

29. **Velikovsky claimed that Mars, like the Moon, was subjected to interplanetary discharges and would exhibit localized areas of stronger than normal radioactivity. This was unexpected by the scientific establishment.** Nevertheless, hot spots were detected on Mars' surface by Mariner IX (1972) and ascribed to radioactivity.

Jupiter

30. **Velikovsky claimed Jupiter had a large magnetic field and that it would emit radio noises of a non-thermal nature. In 1955, B. E Burke and K. L. Franklin of the Carnegie Institute announced, on April 5th, the chance detection of strong radio signals emanating from Jupiter, believed at that time to be a cold body incased in thousands of miles of ice.** In 1960, "V. Radhakrishnah of India and J. A. Roberts of Australia, working at the California Institute of Technology, established the existence of a radiation belt encompassing Jupiter, giving 10 to the 14th power times as much radio energy as the Van Allen belts around the earth." (V. Gargmann and L. Motz: *Science*, vol. 138, December 21, 1962, pp. 1350-1352.)

31. **Velikovsky claimed Jupiter was a dark star. Therefore, it would have an internal heat engine. The astronomical community all through the 1950s – 60s into the 70s said Jupiter was encased in thousands of mile of ice.** (See Charles Ginenthal: »A Tale of Two Venuses«, *The Velikovskian*, Vol. IV, No. 2, 1998, pp. 78-81.) Jupiter is now considered to be a dark star with a great internal source of heat as claimed by G. Kuiper among others. (See D. McNally: »Radio Emissions from the Planet Jupiter«, *Sci Progress*, vol. 53, 1965, pp. 257-262, and P. Peeples: »Are the Interiors of Jupiter and Saturn Hot?«, *The Origin and Evolution of Atmospheres and Oceans* (Brancazic and A. Cameron, eds.), 1964, and A.G. Smith: »Jupiter, the Radio-Active Planet«, *American Scientists*, vol. 57, 1969, pp. 177-192)

Earth

32. **Velikovsky claimed that the Earth had a magnetosphere that reaches at least as far as the Moon. The magnetosphere was discovered by Van Allen and was found to extend far from the Earth.** Critics of Velikovsky claimed he was wrong because the Van Allen Belts did not reach to the Moon. In November 1964, Ness reported on the anti-solar side of the Earth the magnetosphere reaches the Moon. In 1965, Mariner IV, on its way toward Mars, detected Earth's magnetic field at a distance 13 times the radius of the Moon's orbit. In 1971, the Russian Mars 3 Probe proved that it reached 49 times the distance of the Moon from the Earth.

33. **Velikovsky claimed that all petroleum was not biogenic.** Recently Swedish researchers have have managed to prove that fossils from animals and plants are not necessary for crude oil and natural gas to be generated. See Anton Kolesnikov, Vladimir G. Kutcherov, Alexander F. Goncharov: »Methane-derived hydrocarbons produced under upper-mantle conditions«, *Nature Geoscience*, 2009; 2 (8): 566

There are at least 40 more such vindications of Velikovsky's claims as listed in Charles Ginenthal's *Carl Sagan & Immanuel Velikovsky*, Tempe, AZ, 1995, as well as in volumes I through IV of the journal *The Velikovskian*.

High Level Velikovsky
By C. J. Ransom, Ph.D.

Introduction

Catherine Cesarsky, former president of the International Astronomical Union and former director general of the European Southern Observatory (ESO), said in 2009, "The best way to escape [the] bandwagon effect is to look at things from a distance, to connect different ideas." Seeing things from a distance is also called the aerial view or the high level approach. Seeing things from a distance can include analyzing information that is not directly in your field of specialization.

For eight years, Cesarsky tried to change the European Southern Observatory to be more open to unconventional ideas. She said about the result, "I don't think it worked." [Bhattacharjee] Even in light of successes stemming from unconventional ideas, including Velikovsky's, the scientific world often prefers adding decimal places in conventional cosmological theories instead of considering unconventional ideas that have a solid basis in plasma science.

It may sound like a conspiracy but it is not. If you want to obtain your degree or obtain funding for your project, you avoid originality requiring a significant change in accepted ideas. You propose projects to refine ideas that are based on the accepted theory. The projects are then more likely to be approved by the proponents of the accepted theory who control the funding and degrees. That is why it has been so difficult for the scientific community to realize that there is a well established scientific connection to the following questions:

Why did numerous diverse ancient cultures develop similar myths, beliefs and symbols associated with those beliefs?

Why were these beliefs taken so seriously as to require human sacrifices?

Why did these ancient cultures worship planets that are only dots of light in the sky today?

Why did ancient cultures fear comets?

Why can rock art symbols be reproduced in a plasma physics laboratory?

Why do these questions have nothing to do with the supernatural?

Why are all of these questions related?

Velikovsky saw things from a high level and connected the previous questions. The previous questions are related because of plasma images and activities in the ancient sky.

In 1950 Dr. Immanuel Velikovsky wrote *Worlds in Collision* in which he noted that mythology contained information about real world observations. He said that those observations indicated that the ancient sky was different. From the observational data, he also concluded that electromagnetic fields played a major part in the activities that people in various ancient cultures saw in the different ancient sky. The data indicated that occasionally the activities occurring in the sky created havoc on Earth. In addition, he noted that various cultures associated some of those activities with specific planets.

In a later book, *Earth in Upheaval*, Velikovsky used no mythology but only geological data to support the idea that catastrophes had occurred throughout the history of the Earth, no matter how old the Earth was. In that book, Velikovsky even introduced the concept of "Catastrophic Evolution". He concluded that the theory of evolution is vindicated by catastrophic events. He said, "The real enemy of the theory of evolution is the teaching of uniformity, or the non-occurrence of any extraordinary events in the past" [Velikovsky 1955, Ch. 15]. Later, Gould used the term "punctuated equilibrium". This terminology, which described the same concept as catastrophic evolution, allowed Gould to avoid connection with Velikovsky. Unfortunately, this was necessary at the time in order to have the idea considered by mainstream scientists. Now mainstream scientists are sure that global catastrophes did occur throughout Earth's history.

Opponents of Velikovsky in 1950 claimed that his ideas were completely unfounded because of four supposedly known facts:

1. The Solar System was formed in its present state several billion years ago;

2. Electromagnetic fields do not play an important part in the Solar System;

3. Mythology was known to be pure fiction;

4. No sudden events of global nature had ever occurred on Earth.

If those assumptions were really facts, then you could easily see why the believers of those assumptions would suggest that Velikovsky was wrong. Items one through four, however, were only assumptions, and Velikovsky's opponents are now known to have been wrong about all four of those assumptions.

In order to understand the magnitude of the controversy, and partly why it took so long for additional mainstream scientists to study the field of ancient catastrophes, it is important to know that those four statements were the prevailing assumptions of 1950 and were almost articles of faith.

It took about twenty-five years after 1950 before there was widespread acceptance among geologists that item 4) above was incorrect. Today someone who said that no sudden events of global nature had ever occurred on Earth would be treated the way Velikovsky was treated when he wrote *Earth in Upheaval.* It is now clear that Velikovsky was correct that sudden global events occurred throughout the history of Earth. The only disagreement now is when the last event occurred that was visible from most of Earth.

After geologists determined that global catastrophes had occurred throughout the life of Earth, most geologists preferred to assume that nothing major had happened for millions of years. Velikovsky, in 1950, and a number of comparative mythologists and some astronomers more recently, have said that a major global event or events occurred while humans were alive.

In 1950, geologists said Velikovsky was wrong because there had never been a global catastrophe on Earth. By 1979, geologists said there were global catastrophes on Earth, but never within the time of humans. Now geologists are saying that there is a "peer-reviewed collection of papers focusing on the potential of myth storylines to yield data and lessons that are of value to the geological sciences." [Piccardi] The myths were not about normal erosion. From 1950 to 2007 may be a short time in geological time, but it is apparent that the geologists are finally noticing the real world.

Numerous articles and books have been written about the way the academic world mistreated Velikovsky. The fact that the academic world mistreated Velikovsky by attacking the person and irrationally attacking his work does not mean that Velikovsky was right. It also does not mean he was wrong. This article is about more than just describing scientists behaving badly. This article demonstrates that the assumptions used by those who attacked Velikovsky's work were wrong and that many of the conclusions based on their assumptions were wrong. This also does not prove that he was correct, but it certainly demonstrates that the case against him was irrational and weak.

The main premise of this article is that Velikovsky was correct when he suggested that Neolithic/Bronze Age people saw events in the sky that are not seen in the sky today and that observations of those events led to many myths and traditions of the modern world. Whatever events the ancients witnessed, the visions resulted from natural causes that should be, and most likely can be, explained by current scientific methods. Plasma science provides a physical foundation for Velikovsky's assumption that the stories from the ancient world contained information collected through observations of the ancient sky.

The ancients did not create fictional mythology purely from their imaginations. The ancients were a scientifically illiterate people who described natural activities they saw occurring in the sky, but used terms now associated with the supernatural. After the sky changed, people no longer saw those images and activities and incorrectly concluded that the ancient stories were all fictional stories.

The images from plasma science (defined later) and petroglyphs are nearly identical. After one realizes that the ancients saw natural images in the sky that are not there today, it is an easy step to realize that those images were also the inspiration for mythology.

This article is not intended to support Velikovsky's or anyone else's detailed interpretation or model of what the ancients saw. It is intended to support Velikovsky's idea that the ancient sky had images that are not there now and those images and associated motions and changes of those images inspired mythology. It is reasonable to try to interpret scientific data, ancient symbols and ancient writings in terms of something that occurred in the sky that is not occurring there now.

For major information such as the plasma work by Peratt, I supply the original journal reference. In order to reduce clutter and increase readability, I do not provide references for things that I have reason to believe are fairly widely known in certain communities, or those of side interest.

It is not significant for this discussion whether or not Velikovsky was wrong about some details about ancient catastrophes, just as it is not significant that Darwin was wrong about some details of evolution. The important idea is that both men had correct high level concepts.

Top-Down Bottom-Up

In the computer world, there are two major terms applied to software development. These terms are "top-down" and "bottom-up" development. In bottom-up, numerous details are grouped, sorted and correlated to eventually lead to a comprehensive program with major sections. This is the approach scientific experimental research often uses. In top-down, the major sections are developed and then the details are added.

In practice, software developers, as well as writers, and scientists, use a combination of top-down and bottom-up. Professors tell writers to make an outline before starting to write an essay, book or article. That is top-down. That can be done only if you have enough details to decide how to construct the outline. People who developed comprehensive models of the recent history of the Solar System initially used the bottom-up approach, developed the top-down concepts and then added additional details.

Part of the problem in discussing a comprehensive hypothesis is that proponents may be discussing one level of the hypothesis without realizing that the opposition is discussing another level of the hypothesis. One side may present evidence for a top level concept and the other side may present evidence that appears to refute a detail that is merely a secondary conclusion of the higher level concept. The secondary conclusion may be only one of many possibilities that may result from the top level concept. It often does not matter that one or more secondary conclusions are false.

Sometimes people realize they are arguing at a different level and continue to do so intentionally. In that case, the objective is not to determine an accurate solution, but to retain one's status or win the argument. This happens in politics as well as science.

Arguing at different levels is easier for each side, but is hardly productive. It is sometimes difficult to analyze a model in enough detail to understand what is a very important concept, and what is an interesting but marginal speculation. People whose main interest is ridiculing anyone else's idea or merely having another publication may prefer to argue at different levels. They do not care about discerning top level concepts from secondary details. In that case, both sides can appear right and prove their point without having to concede much to the other side. This approach sometimes seems to be preferred in the academic world.

The following is an example of a minor secondary detail that is wrong, but it does not make any difference to the major idea:

Based on Benjamin Franklin's observations about lightning, he said that the tip of a lightning rod should be pointed. A team from the Langmuir Laboratory for Atmospheric Research at the New Mexico Institute of Mining and Technology performed research indicating that blunt tops were better for lightning rods. The pointed tip rods worked when no other lightning rods were around, but did not receive lightning strikes when both pointed and blunt rods were in the same area.

Franklin was right about the need for lightning rods, but wrong about the shape. This seems to be a minor point, so to speak, if a non-blunt lightning rod protected your building from damage by lightning. However, this is the type of minor point that one group uses as proof that another group is wrong. One side would argue that Franklin was wrong about needing a sharp point. The other side would argue that Franklin was right about lightning rods being useful. Both sides would be essentially correct. In the academic world, the winner of the discussion would be the person with the most influence at the time. The influence could range from stopping a student from graduating or eliminating funding for a rival's research program.

Although more famous for being a science fiction writer, James P. Hogan wrote several non-fiction books. In 2004, he wrote *Kicking the Sacred Cow*. In one section he outlined and supported several of

Velikovsky's points. In that section, he also noted someone else who had the details wrong but the concept right, and that person is as famous as Franklin. Hogan said, "Copernicus didn't have all the details right either – he got the Sun in the center but thought the planets moved on circles rather than ellipses – but that doesn't diminish what we refer to today as the Copernican revolution" [Hogan].

Similarly, Velikovsky had some details wrong, but that does not diminish his contribution to the high level understanding of the recent history of the Solar System.

For some issues, people on both sides of the recent catastrophe concept have discussed items at too detailed a level. Each side made fun of the other side's abilities, and each side may have been correct about the particular point being discussed. However, the point really did not affect the overall argument about whether Velikovsky's high level concepts are correct or incorrect.

Velikovsky analyzed thousands of details about ancient mythology. Based on this analysis, he made five top level conclusions:

1. The appearance of the sky underwent noticeable changes within the time of people.
2. The images and activities in the ancient sky inspired mythology.
3. Electromagnetic fields played a significant part in the appearance of the Solar System to the ancients.
4. Catastrophes of a global nature impacted at least the environment on the Earth and possibly some geological structures.
5. A detailed model of the recent history of the Solar System can be enhanced using data from mythology.

As demonstrated below, Velikovsky was right about these high level concepts.

Scope

I will address in detail the first three of Velikovsky's top level concepts and a small portion of the fourth.

I address 1-3 because I have studied plasma science and details about potential models of the ancient sky for over forty years. I am familiar with most of the arguments for and against changes in the ancient sky and the effects of electromagnetic fields and their involvement in the Universe. I address a small portion of 4 because of the overlap in some areas of physics.

A number of authors address 5 and I do not cover that item in this article. Item 5 contains so many variables that it is difficult if not impossible to determine an exact model. Several similar models may be generally correct and still have some incorrect details.

A number of people who study comparative mythology agree that useful information can be determined by comparing myths. A typical comment is, "However, as I have discussed earlier, by careful historical comparison we can isolate certain motifs, individual myths, and even whole myth complexes both in time and space, compare them, and try to trace their common origin" [Witzel].

Some of those comparative mythologists agree with Velikovsky's top level concept that the common origin may be images in the sky and that a detailed model of what the ancients saw can be determined from comparative mythology. They, however, do not agree with the details of his model. These people include Dwardu Cardona, Dave Talbott and Ev Cochrane. These people even disagree among themselves about details of the models of the ancient sky. The subject is extremely complex and I have not investigated this area enough to make judgments. For details of various models, see the works by Velikovsky, Cardona, Talbott and Cochrane. Other people also have models involving recent changes in the Solar System. **This paper does not address any of those models.**

I believe that if Velikovsky were alive now, he would be one of the leaders in modifying the details of item 5. In fact, Velikovsky supplied the basic ideas behind the models by Cardona, Talbott and Cochrane. I believe Velikovsky would have developed those ideas further had he lived longer and not had to waste time replying to irrational comments from the academic community.

People can independently conclude with ease that the ancients saw something in the sky that is not there today, that mythology contains useful scientific information, and that an image appearing as a comet played an important part in the events of early people. Some authors who predated Velikovsky in the 18th and 19th centuries apparently independently formed those conclusions, and some of the authors who wrote after Velikovsky published his major works may have easily developed the ideas independently because of the abundance of data. In the academic world, it was not considered proper to read Velikovsky so many researchers may not have done so and may have independently developed the ideas. In some cases, it is clear that for political reasons people expanded Velikovsky's work without mentioning Velikovsky. In either case, it is clear that numerous modern investigators have reason to believe that the ancient sky was different.

Primeval Plasma Pictures

Plasma is sometimes called the fourth state of matter. Solids are first, then liquids, gases and plasma. Plasma is more likely the first state of matter. When plasma loses energy, or cools, it becomes a gas. When gas cools, it becomes liquid. When liquid cools, it becomes solid. The sequence is usually mentioned in the opposite direction because on Earth, that is the most common observation. When energy is added to a solid, the solid becomes a liquid, etc. The Universe is considered to be about 99% plasma and losing energy; hence, plasma can be considered the first state of matter.

Neon signs, fluorescent lights, and lightning are plasma or plasma discharges. Plasmas are very common beyond the Earth's atmosphere. For example, the Sun, solar wind, stars and nebulae are plasmas.

The Earth's polar auroras are natural plasmas. The auroras have been observed with awe for centuries. Kristian Birkeland, who investigated "ionized gases" over a century ago before the term plasma was coined, was the first to claim that a plasma effect was the cause of the auroras.

A coronal mass ejection (CME) is plasma that can affect the intensity of the aurora. Although the auroras are not visible in the lower latitudes today, a CME in 1859 was so intense that the aurora was visible as far south as Central America and northern South America. It is easy to understand how impressive it would be to ancient cultures to have an exceptional aurora that may have lasted for years.

Plasma in nature or in the laboratory can take on many shapes. The properties of plasma scale over many orders of magnitude, so effects seen in the sky can often be scaled down and reproduced in the laboratory. Inversely, effects seen in the laboratory can be expected to be found in the Universe on a very large scale.

Process

There are several steps to the process of demonstrating that the ancient sky was different from today's sky. Those steps need to provide support for the following:

A. Prehistoric rock art reproduced images that could have been seen in the ancient sky,

B. Early myths, first oral and later written, mimic images and activities that could have been seen in the ancient sky.

Each of these, if true, strongly suggests that the ancient sky was different.

Point A can be demonstrated in the laboratory by plasma science. Plasma forms can be directly correlated with ancient petroglyphs. This correlation is strong support for the idea that the view from Earth of the ancient sky was different. This does not rely on myths that were written considerably after the disappearance of the plasma. That the plasma must have been visible worldwide to inspire similar rock art throughout the world demonstrates that the ancient sky was different and the plasma was not just a local phenomenon.

The people of antiquity were not a homogeneous entity or a monolithic unit. The differences between the various cultural perceptions strongly argue against there being one original culture or one original language from which the global images and stories of myths could have derived. On the other hand, various non-interacting cultures created many unusual but similar images and stories about those images. This is easily understandable if the diverse cultures saw similar images and activities in the sky (Point B). Cross-reference support is that many images in myths, such as the world-mountain and ladder of heaven, correlate with images in rock art.

Basic Plasma Correlation

Point A involves correlating ancient drawings to a natural phenomenon that could have occurred in the ancient sky. Anthony Peratt has correlated images of plasma discharges in a modern plasma laboratory with ancient petroglyphs. This correlation strongly indicates that many diverse early cultures saw the images in natural plasma in the sky. The once easily seen visible plasma phenomenon is not there now.

Dr. Peratt is a plasma scientist at the Los Alamos National Laboratory in New Mexico. Scientists there and at other laboratories sometimes study Earth's aurora, called the Aurora Borealis or Northern Lights in the northern hemisphere, to determine more about space particles encountering Earth and the effect on Earth's plasma environment and upper atmosphere. The aurora provides information to compare to laboratory experiments and computer simulations.

Through various discussions about petroglyphs and their origin, he realized that there was a strong correlation between images in his laboratory plasma, the images that would be produced in a strong aurora, and images in the petroglyphs and ancient symbols. After this realization, he started studying petroglyphs and enlisted help from people around the world to take measurements of images. Measurements included type, location (GPS), orientation and field of view. He published some of his findings in »Characteristics for the Occurrence of a High-Current, Z-Pinch Aurora as Recorded in Antiquity«, which was in the *IEEE Transactions on Plasma Science* in 2003 [Peratt, 2003]. Peratt's work clearly indicates that there was something different, but natural, visible in the ancient sky.

Peratt's and other researchers' plasma science laboratory experiments produce images similar to ancient petroglyphs. Some images, when reduced to the same scale, are exact overlays. One type of plasma used in the experiments, called a Z-pinch, is the same type of plasma that produces the aurora at the poles.

Analysis of tens of thousands of petroglyphs indicates that the people who drew ancient petroglyphs almost always had a clear view toward the north or south. This commonality of view and identity of rock art and laboratory images indicate the ancients drew images they saw emanating near the magnetic poles. This, in turn, provides support for the assumption that the ancients were taking data instead of being creative while drawing symbols and composing myths. It gives a physical foundation for considering that the ancient sky was not the same as the sky we see today. If these distinct images appeared in the ancient sky, then myths and ancient symbols become understandable data.

For example, the ancients drew stick figures thought to represent humans. The stick figures appear in a number of odd configurations. Sometimes the figures have a dot on one or both sides of the torso, other times there are extra legs, sometimes extra arms, and sometimes the figures are wearing fancy headdresses or have smaller humans or animals by their sides. All of these images and more are found both in rock art and in the plasmas created in laboratories.

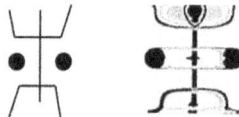

Figure 1   Representation of Squatter petroglyph and plasma
(Plasma from Peratt's Figure 32)

Squatter images are found throughout the world. The similarities are so striking that researchers, who have not heard of the plasma possibility, assume that the squatter figure must have spread with the population. For example, Breuer said, "Otherwise how can the similarity be explained between the black and white painted bowls from Kansu, China and those from New Mexico and Arizona" [Breuer]. He provided drawings of the figures, as simulated in Figure 2, and all three fit the squatter category. Peratt's plasma model also explains why there are lightning-like fingers and toes not numbering five. The caption to his figure 41 says, "Example of an electrical discharge that has formed two filamentary currents each of which trifurcate at the bottom to allow the conduction of the current carried in the filaments." The picture of the electrical current closely resembles the three fingers or toes found on many petroglyphs.

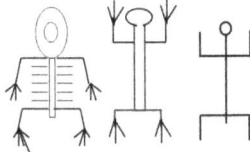

Figure 2 Squatters from China, New Mexico and Arizona (After Breuer)

From the plasma information presented by Peratt it is reasonable to conclude that the ancients drew stick figure representations of what they saw in plasmas high above the surface of Earth. Additional examples and correlations follow. There is no need to resort to visitors from space to explain the odd shapes, and there is no need to resort to diffusion to explain the worldwide similarity.

Natural Phenomena Inspired Rock Art

If art is communication, then petroglyphs represent communication from some of our earliest ancestors. We have ignored what they tried to tell us.

We call the people who carved petroglyphs primitive because we consider ourselves so advanced that we believe they could not have seen what they drew. We see their scribbles, lines, circles and sometimes something that looks like an alien or an animal. Since we do not understand the scribbles, lines, circles or alien looking pictures today we believe the ancients were untalented or taking drugs. We interpret the symbols in a way that agrees with our beliefs of how intelligent the artists must have been and what they could have seen in the ancient sky.

If the ancient skies were different and the ancients drew what they saw in the sky, you could expect to find some worldwide similarities in rock art. Emmanuel Anati was a Professor of Palaeo-ethnology at the

University of Lecce, Italy. He founded the International Committee on Rock Art (CAR) of the International Council on Monuments and Sites (ICOMOS). Anati noted that rock art throughout the world has similar associations and symbolism.

Anati attributes this similarity to a previous "primordial mother language." Opponents said that this primordial language would have to have been around for nearly a million years for it to create the universal rock art. However, a primordial language would not be needed if all the ancients observed the same images in the sky and reproduced those images as rock art.

Dr. E. Devlet of the Institute of Archaeology, Russian Academy of Sciences in Moscow, not only noted the widespread similarity of ancient rock art, he suggested an astronomical influence. He said, "Numerous and mysterious geometrical signs of rock art demonstrate an external formal similarity and have a wide territorial and chronological spread." Also, "In some cases such figures may be interpreted as images of astronomical objects" [Devlet].

Devlet assumes that the astronomical objects are visible today, but this is not necessarily the case. However, it is clear from the work of Anati, Devlet and others that there are a number of ancient universal rock symbols.

Correlating meaning in petroglyphs depends on *who drew what,* and *when they drew it.* With proper dating of ancient rock drawings, it may be easier to discern which symbols originated simultaneously, which were drawn later to carry on the culture, and which diffused as attempts to disseminate the culture. Unfortunately, there is currently not a fully accepted dating technique for rock art.

There recently was a technique that was used to provide the generally accepted dates of various rock art depictions. The originator of this technique was very influential. Some people were ridiculed when they disagreed with the dates provided by that researcher. The fact that it was difficult if not impossible for others to reproduce the researcher's results was often ignored because he influenced the field so greatly. Eventually, others decided that the researcher was *adjusting* the experiment to make it provide the desired dates. Of course that created an extensive controversy [Bednarik]. (Influential authorities also claimed that Velikovsky was wrong. Those authorities were later proved to be wrong.)

The result is that there is no currently accepted accurate technique for dating all rock art, and the dates developed over the last fifteen years are now questionable. The whole field of rock art analysis can be a very fruitful field for interested parties.

Although it is not currently possible to provide all petroglyphs with an absolute date, there are some techniques that can provide some useful estimates.

Scott and Peratt presented »The Origin of Petroglyphs – Recordings of a Catastrophic Aurora in Human Prehistory?« at the International Conference on Plasma Science in Jeju, Korea during June 2-5, 2003. They said that the purpose of the paper was "an attempt to explain how in man's prehistory recordings of high-energy-density phenomena could have been carved on rock in an accurate, systematic, and apparently temporally accurate fashion" [Scott, 2003].

This was part of work originated by Peratt and published in December of 2003. In his paper »Characteristics for the Occurrence of a High-Current, Z-Pinch Aurora as Recorded in Antiquity«, Peratt limited the study to petroglyphs thought to range in age from 10,000 to 2000 BCE. He was able to find the approximate date of some of the petroglyphs because investigators determined the age by analyzing items buried slightly above the petroglyphs.

Workers removed a meter of soil from the Glorieta Mesa and Rowe Mesa horizontal petroglyph sites near Santa Fe, NM, USA. Analysis of campfire debris a few centimeters above the petroglyphs indicated that the petroglyphs were at least 4000 years old. Peratt also used data from New Mexico, Texas, California, Utah, Arizona, Nevada, Colorado, Oregon, Idaho, Washington, and British Columbia, Canada, as well as data from other locations throughout the world.

He mostly analyzed petroglyphs where he knew the GPS longitude/latitude positions and orientation with respect to the most probable field-of-view. Peratt suggested the line-of-sight to the Earth's magnetic poles is one reason petroglyphs are often carved in difficult or specialized locations when equally satisfactory rocks in more readily accessible locations are in the same area.

During the analysis, Peratt identified eighty-four distinct high-energy-density Z-pinch patterns that have been found in petroglyphs. He determined that a large percentage of petroglyphs could be classified corresponding with plasma data. Only a small percentage of the petroglyphs analyzed do not fall into any of these plasma categories.

The type of plasma he analyzed is called a Z-pinch. A Z-pinch could look similar to a funnel with the tube portion pointed toward Earth's magnetic pole. (Figure 3) Much of the funnel would be visible because of light emission by the plasma. The color changes as the conditions in the upper atmosphere and height above the Earth change. The non-white aurora colors are mostly green, red, and blue. Sometimes red and green overlap and produce yellow. As the conditions change, the plasma produces different images. The changing conditions caused the images to appear to be active entities.

Figure 3 Funnel shape of Z-pinch plasma at magnetic pole.

Peratt suggested that an intense aurora could have created the patterns found in petroglyphs. He also suggested that an event of that type could have been produced if the solar wind had increased only one or two orders of magnitude from what it is today. Some of Peratt's experimental data, simulation data and petroglyph comparisons follow.

Figure 4 depicts plasma simulation, plasma experiment and petroglyph data. The first two views (A) are simulations as time progresses. The third view (B) is of the experimental plasma. The fourth view (C) is a petroglyph called a ladder, and the fifth view (D) is a petroglyph called a caterpillar. The change from ladder to caterpillar corresponds to the time change of the electrical current in the plasma. Ladders and caterpillar petroglyphs are found worldwide.

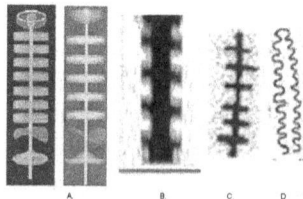

Figure 4 A. Two times during simulation, B. experiment, C. ladder petroglyph, D. caterpillar petroglyph. From Peratt's Fig. 9 and Fig. 22.

A number of ancient myths mention a stairway to the stars or stairway to heaven. A commonly known term is Jacob's Ladder, which describes a ladder to heaven. "He [Jacob] had a dream, and behold, a ladder was set on the earth with its top reaching to heaven; and behold, the angels of God were ascending and descending on it" [Genesis 28:12]. Numerous other ancient stories describe the leader of a group ascending to heaven on a ladder.

Figure 5 Amulet of the Ladder

The Egyptians had a ladder-shaped amulet (Figure 5). "In tombs of the Ancient and Middle Empires small objects of wood and other substances in the form of ladders have often been found, but the signification of them is not always apparent" [Budge, p. 51]. Budge also said that the ladder was often placed on or near the deceased and it appeared that it was supposed to be used to climb to heaven.

Striations, dark gaps between the light-emitting pockets of gas, are common in a number of plasmas. A fluorescent light is a type of plasma. As the tube ages, the conditions change and sometimes striations can be seen in the light. If the tube were vertical, in some cases the striations could resemble a ladder. Depending on the conditions, the striations can be stationary or moving. Plasma of this nature in the sky could give the impression of an escalator to heaven. Of course, ancient people did not know about escalators, and those people represented it as flowing or falling water. It seems reasonable that some type of striated plasma effect could have been seen in the ancient sky. If so, this would probably have been a very impressive sight. It would have been uncommon and, hence, worthy of drawings and stories.

It seems reasonable that the original stairway or ladder to heaven was so impressive that the terminology was handed down for generations and was the origin of some of the creative titles of today. Most people may not realize that the songs *Stairway to the Stars* and *Stairway to Heaven* and the electrically generated effect called Jacob's

Ladder, often shown in mad scientist movies, may have ancient counterparts.

Professor Roger Williams Wescott received his Ph. D. in Linguistics from Princeton in 1948. Among other things, he taught Folklore and Comparative Religion and served as President of the International Society for the Comparative Study of Civilizations. In one of his forty books, he noted that throughout the world the main god was sometimes pictured as being at the top of a ladder, creating an image that has become known as the *world axis*. This was considered a living link between Heaven and Earth.

Figure 6 Sun symbol, Sun symbol on ladder

Often the *sun* symbol, such as in Figure 6 A, representing the main god, was depicted on top of a ladder or stairway similar to the one in Figure 4 C. Sometimes the ladder did not have a line through the center of the steps, but had lines on the sides like a modern ladder, such as in Figure 6 B. Sometimes the horizontal lines did not have vertical lines attached such as Figure 6 C. Wescott speculated that an image of this nature might have been created through a plasma mechanism similar to what is currently thought to be a plasma flux-tube connecting Jupiter and its satellite Io [Wescott].

Figure 7 Older and later forms of Egyptian Symbol Tet and the Ankh

The older form of the Egyptian symbol called Tet or Djed is a column with four cross pieces near the top (Figure 7). In the *Concept of the Djed Symbol*, Vincent Brown said the symbol Tet is considered one of the most mysterious. Sir Alan H. Gardiner was one of the premier

Egyptologists of the early twentieth century. Brown noted that Gardiner referred to the lines as vertebrae. After additional comments from various people, Brown said, "From the descriptions above, it can be understood that the general concept of the Djed symbol appears to be a combination of the backbone of Osiris, a column or pillar, and the trunk of a tree" [V. Brown]. All of these descriptions would also fit a plasma column from the sky to Earth such as described by Peratt.

Budge said that in some cases, the Tet supports the amulet of life, called the Ankh. [Budge, p. 58]. The Ankh is a cross with an oval at the top. This sign represents the plasma column with either a spheroidal-shaped plasma called a plasmoid or a solid body within the plasma. Some of the models of the ancient sky indicate that the spheroid at the top of the life symbol represented the universal god.

In the late nineteenth century, Birkeland discovered twisted corkscrew shaped paths taken by electric currents in air or in a near vacuum. He found that electric currents move through space largely by means of electrons spiraling along magnetic field lines. These currents are often called Birkeland currents, but sometimes they are called field-aligned currents. They most often occur in pairs. These pairs tend to compress between them any ionized or neutral material in the plasma. Sometimes those twisted shapes are easily visible to the unaided eye and sometimes they are not. When visible, these twisted pairs of current look like snakes or twisted intertwined ropes. Peratt gives an example of Birkeland currents as the charged particle electrical currents streaming up and down the aurora at the magnetic pole.

Figure 8 Birkeland current appearing petroglyphs, Jeffers, MN, USA
(Photo by Anita Ransom)

Symbols of this type (Figure 8) are often found in ancient art as just the ropes, but sometimes associated with other symbols. The ropes are often represented as snakes. It is easy to see why the ancients, if they saw an exceptionally active aurora, would associate Birkeland currents with snakes.

The Caduceus has evolved into the current symbol that is often used in connection with the medical profession. An earlier appearance of this symbol did not have the wings. There was only a pole in the middle, and the pole often had a sphere at the top. The ropes or snakes entwined around the pole (Figure 9).

Figure 9 Early Caduceus

The relationship of the early Caduceus symbol to mythology is presented in the section about the Cosmic Tree.

Peratt said that one of the important classes of petroglyphs he did not discuss in his paper was the spiral. The spiral petroglyphs can resemble a galaxy. In some of my earlier research, I observed spirals in plasmas [Ransom 1963].

Figure 10 Spiral types found in plasma contained in a magnetic bottle

The spirals depicted in Figure 10 were seen in plasmas generated in a cylindrical glass tube immersed within what is called a magnetic bottle with the magnetic field lines along the axis of the tube. Viewing the end of the cylinder under certain gas pressure, magnetic field and electric field conditions, one can see the stationary spiral. Depending on the conditions, the spiral can have three, four, five or more arms. All of these spirals in the plasma are similar to those seen in ancient art all over the world. A rock picture stone from Gotland, Sweden looks surprisingly like the six-arm spiral in figure 10 [Graves].

As the magnetic field changed, the three-arm spiral depicted in Figure 10 changed the number of arms. The magnetic field for the stable spirals was usually between 200 and 300 gauss measured at the center of the front magnetic coil. Stable spirals would appear about 20 gauss apart. Sometimes the spiral would not be stable but could be seen on film from a high-speed camera that used about 30 meters of film a second.

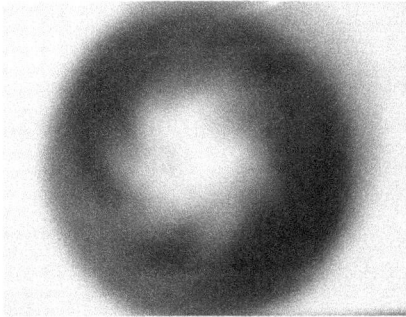

Figure 11   Picture of plasma containing six-arm spiral
(Photo by C. J. Ransom)

The first spiral to be seen had three arms. As the magnetic field increased, the three-arm spiral would disappear. With additional increase in the magnetic field, a stable spiral with four arms would appear. As the magnetic field increased further, the four arms would disappear and then five arms would appear. Above five arms, the spiral would appear more like a bright circular saw blade on a dark background. Figure 11 shows a picture of the six-arm spiral in the plasma. The picture was taken with a high-speed camera.

Peratt's correlation can be looked at two ways. Since non-interacting cultures drew similar images, those cultures were probably inspired by the same view. An obvious location for that view is the sky. From the other viewpoint, if non-interacting cultures saw the same images in the sky, it is reasonable to assume that they would draw similar images. This is further supported by the unusual nature of some of the images.

The events causing the images in the ancient sky were natural, and definitely were not supernatural, but they were very unusual. They were unusual not because the events were merely recurring events that just do not happen often, such as floods or earthquakes. The conditions creating the ancient unusual events have completely changed, and conditions are no longer appropriate to produce those events today. We are not likely to see a time where the gods are visible in the sky again.

Myths Mimic Sky Image Activity

In supporting point A we mentioned comparing only experimental plasma physics images and images produced by ancient people. That does not require the inclusion of written statements from the ancients. Point B ("Early myths, first oral and later written, mimic images and activities seen in the ancient sky") requires investigation of the words the ancients associated with certain images. This area is more open to interpretation than the comparison of experimental images to petroglyphs; however, there is no doubt about the worldwide similarity of some ancient myths.

Professor Michael Grant and John Hazel said, "Everyone who compares the Greek and Roman mythologies with those of other cultures throughout the various countries of the world, and throughout the successive periods of history, will be amazed, indeed staggered, by the frequency with which the same stories recur, in closely similar or identical form, in a vast number of different lands, times and contexts" [Grant]. They mention the two popular ideas of why this is true, diffusion and one primordial language, but indicate problems with both explanations. They do not mention the possibility that everyone saw the same video in the sky about the same time and created similar descriptions.

Several comparative mythologists have correlated worldwide symbols and myths and identified basic archetypes in the data. A subset of those comparative mythologists noticed the worldwide correlation, but did not associate the correlated events with activities in the ancient sky. Another subset of the comparative mythologists realized that the ancients claimed those archetypes and activities were in the ancient sky (Point B). Some Neolithic/Bronze Age people reproduced the archetype images on rocks and pottery.

Writing is thought to have been invented primarily for economic reasons, especially in Mesopotamia where the earliest records are bookkeeping records. A few individual characters, however, may have been based on the cosmic images. Those images permanently recorded the data about the ancient sky. For example, some researchers concluded that "sun" images in China, on the Neolithic pottery from the Da-wenkou culture (about 3000 BCE and earlier) could have been the basis of primitive Chinese script [Singh].

To enhance the support of points A and B, researchers need to accomplish a number of sub-activities. Three of these are

1) create one or more models about what was different,
2) develop physical explanations for those models,
3) compare the models to what is discovered in the Solar System by space probes.

No one has demonstrated all the points and all the additional sub-activities.

The following is support for the high level concept that early myths, first oral and later written, mimic images and activities seen in the ancient sky.

Astronomers Victor Clube and Bill Napier wrote *The Cosmic Winter* in 1990. They said that the ancients saw a night sky, "*which is not the one we see now*" (Original in italics) [Clube 1990, p. 78]. Clube and Napier are not the only ones in the academic field to claim, based on comparative mythology, that the ancient sky was different.

Astronomer Duncan Steel wrote *Marking Time* about why various ancient groups described their histories as they related to major epochs that involved catastrophic beginnings or endings. He said, "My opinion is that this was not one discrete event like a multiple planetary conjunction, but rather a continuing phenomenon which persisted for some centuries and that, coupled with the vagaries of myths, legends and the timings associated with them handed down over the generations, led to a spread of start epochs being assigned across the main cultures which witnessed much the same thing" [Steel, 2000, p. 230].

He attributes the multiple events to multiple encounters with objects that gave a considerably different appearance to the ancient sky.

The previous information describes two different approaches to determining the ancient sky was different. One is Peratt's plasma laboratory images compared to ancient symbols approach. The other is the approach that considers myths to be historical anecdotal data instead of pure fiction. That was the approach used by Velikovsky, Clube, Napier, Steel and others.

The principles used in the plasma approach and in the approach using ancient writings as data are opposite in direction, but lead to the same basic conclusion: *The ancient sky was different and events in the ancient sky were very unusual but not un-natural.*

First principles of Peratt's approach using plasma physics:

- Laboratory plasma images are nearly identical to petroglyph images.
- People copied images; they did not create the images from their imaginations.
- Petroglyph images changed as the plasma evolved.
- Ancients from around the world saw the same images from different directions.
- The perspectives of the same images can be analyzed to locate the image in space.
- Space age data indicate that the old concept of nothing unusual having happened is inadequate.

Basic conclusions from plasma approach:

1. The ancient sky was different.
2. Images in the ancient sky inspired similar symbols in different cultures.
3. Events in the ancient sky were unusual but not un-natural.

First principles of approach by Velikovsky and astronomers such as Clube, Napier, Steel and others using ancient myths and symbols as data:

- Ancient documents indicate the ancient sky was different.
- The ancient documents indicate that images in the sky appeared frightening and created havoc on Earth.
- Images and stories evolved as conditions changed.
- People copied images; they did not create the images from their imaginations.
- People created stories about what they considered the personified activities of the images; they did not create the stories from their imaginations.
- Ancients from around the world saw the same images from different directions.
- The ancients localized some of the events and characteristics of the heroes in the stories.
- Space age data indicate that the old concept of nothing unusual having happened is inadequate.

Basic conclusions from correlation or worldwide mythic approach:

1. The ancient sky was different.
2. Images in the ancient sky inspired similar beliefs, rituals and symbols in different cultures.
3. Events in the ancient sky were unusual but not un-natural.

Both approaches give the same result.

Recently, researchers using both approaches made the same major conclusion reached by Velikovsky in 1950: *The ancient sky was not the sky that is seen today, but the events causing the different ancient sky can be explained by modern science.*

Difficult To Correlate

Ancient people created a number of symbols representing objects they saw in the sky. Many of those symbols bear little or no resemblance to what we see in the sky today. For example, nothing in the sky today would present the image of a star within the center of a crescent. Today we think of that symbol as creative artwork, but apparently the ancients did not share that opinion.

Some ancient symbols that supposedly represent the Sun god are not how we would draw the sun. For example, the Sun was sometimes drawn as a wheel – that is, a circle with four spokes and a hub. This *Sun Wheel* symbol was used as a religious symbol even before people used mechanical wheels. Sun wheels played a central role in the Mayan architecture and religious rites from the beginning of Mayan culture although they did not learn to use the mechanical wheel until post-Columbian times.

The ancients associated the images in the ancient sky with the mythology that they developed at that time. The images were not always stationary or isolated objects in the sky. The images moved in unusual ways and interacted with each other. This produced a panoramic view of the gods fighting, loving and playing in the sky. Sometimes the interactions of the gods created havoc on Earth.

Clube and Napier said that the ancients had gods with attributes that are associated with comets. Many comparative mythologists say that the ancient gods were also associated with planets and the plasma interactions among various bodies, including what were called comets, seen in the ancient sky. There are indications that people did not really separate planets and comets from each other until the 1st millennium BCE.

There are two schools of thought about the characteristics of the gods associated with the current planets. One group considers the possibility the polar plasma contained large spherical plasmas called spheroids. After the breakup of the plasma configuration, the characteristics of the gods that were spheroids were transferred to the planets. The other group considers that that some of the planets were originally closer than they are today and that those planets were involved with the plasma configuration. Velikovsky was in that group. In that case, when the orbits of the planets changed, the god characteristics of the planets stayed associated with the planets.

If the plasma configuration contained no planets other than Earth, the plasma may have been bright enough to shield the other planets as well as the stars. When the plasma configuration disappeared, the appearance of the visible planets may have created confusion about the disappearance of the plasma gods. If the planets were always visible in their current orbits, it is doubtful that there would have been confusion about the planets and plasma gods. If there were no confusion caused by the sudden appearance of previously invisible planets, there would be little reason to associate the *plasma only* gods with planets after the breakup of the plasma configuration.

It appears that either the plasma created a situation where the planets were not visible as long as the major plasma configuration existed, or some planets really were closer to Earth and were involved with the plasma. If the planets were not visible in their present orbits, then the god characteristics were transferred to the planets when the planets became visible after the breakup of the plasma configuration. In either case, the stars were probably not visible during the time of the plasma. The possibility that stars were not visible during the polar plasma configuration makes it understandable why the ancient myths describe a time when the stars were created.

Transfer of characteristics to planets could be similar to the situation where the ancients took events seen in the sky and associated the events with local geological features. Also, local rulers often acquired epithets associated with the gods in order to claim being a direct descendant of the gods. Being a direct descendant of the gods supposedly gave the ruler a divine right to rule. The idea of divine right handed down from the plasma gods continued into the current era.

An indication of the problem with analyzing ancient stories is that there are rarely exact correlations that fit a particular identification and only that identification. This would probably be true even if you had access to the original sources. Although Mars is usually the warrior hero, in one culture or another a planet other than Mars may also have some of the characteristics of the mythic warrior. No model of the ancient sky will fit all of the details of all of the ancient stories.

Models may be developed that will explain the past more accurately than what is presently taught, but there might still be data that do not fit the model completely. A model that fits ancient historical data to an extraordinary degree, but still misses some details, is probably closer to what occurred in the past than what is currently taught, i.e., that nothing happened and the ancients were just imaginative.

The earliest observers of the phenomena in the different ancient sky created the early myths. Those observers personified the objects and the activities of those beings in heaven. They saw balls of light, circles of light or spheres of light, crescents of light, lightning, streamers, intertwining streamers, window outlines with vertical blinds, crowns, headdresses, crosses, glowing trees, stick figures, and combinations of those phenomena. Those observers knew nothing about astronomy and nothing about plasma science. They had no way of knowing that what they saw was plasma activity interacting with perhaps asteroids, comets or planets and the objects were not gods playing in the sky.

After the breakup of the extraordinary plasma configuration in the ancient sky, the current configuration of the Solar System became apparent. People several generations later who did not witness the extraordinary activity in the sky assumed that nothing really happened previously and that the Polar regions and the Solar System had always been seen the way the later generations saw them.

It is normal and practical for scientists' first assumption for any theory about the recent history of the Earth or the Solar System to be that nothing unusual happened in the past. If the data fit that theory, then everything is reasonably straightforward. However, much of the data do not fit the theory that nothing unusual happened. There is abundant data indicating that something unusual did happen relatively recently on Earth and in the Solar System. Unfortunately, some scientists try to ignore that data or claim the data do not exist.

Two Common Themes

Two of the most common themes from the ancient data are stories about the sacred tree, world tree, or cosmic tree and about extensive comet activity.

The Cosmic Tree

In the *Dictionary of Symbols*, Tresidder said that the Caduceus was associated with the gods in Phoenicia, Babylon, Egypt and India. The pole represented the *Tree of Life*. This was "a means of communication or route for messages between Earth and sky" [Tresidder, p. 34]. He said that this symbol is over four thousand years old. Ancients throughout the world also seemed to believe that a rope provided a path or *ladder* between heaven and Earth, and that ropes and snakes were often associated with the cosmic serpent [Tresidder, p. 171].

"The World Pillar was associated with various symbolic forms by the ancient sky watchers, one of the most common of which was that of the Cosmic Mountain" [Cochrane, 1997, p. 98]. The *Tree of Life* was another widespread concept in the ancient world. In *Gods and Myths of Northern Europe*, Davidson said, "This world had at its center a great tree, a mighty ash called Yggdrasil. So huge was this tree that its branches stretched out over heaven and earth alike" [Davidson].

The Christmas tree and the Maypole are two representations of the *Tree of Life* in the modern world. The Christmas tree was used in rituals by pagan religions and was absorbed in part of Christian celebrations, but it originated from the plasma configuration. Ancient dances around the Maypole, with its Birkeland-current-appearing twisting ropes, were sometimes accompanied by sacrifices. Many people have seen a similar religious ritual re-enacted in Mexico by Aztec descendents.

Rock art includes symbols that appear to be a pole with one or more spheroids at the top, one or more lines through the pole near the top, one or more snake-like lines around the pole and often an orb-like fruit or flower. This could reasonably be associated with later written descriptions of the sacred tree or cosmic tree. The spheroids sometimes have streamers that may appear as feathers and is associated with one or more birds. The tree also often connects Earth with heaven.

If the inspiration for the petroglyph symbols were in the sky and visible to diverse cultures, it would be reasonable to expect cosmic tree stories from diverse non-interacting cultures. The following indicates a widespread use of a cosmic tree-like feature in many myths and how some of the attributes of the myths relate to the ancient plasma. It is not intended to be an in-depth comparison of myths or a portion of a detailed reconstruction of the activities in the ancient sky.

VanderSluijs notes that the sacred tree symbol is also presented in mythology as a mountain, a pillar, a sacred building, and a 'cosmic man' or world giant [VanderSluijs]. He supports the concept that all of those symbols are related to another mythological term called the world axis or axis mundi. The term "axis mundi" apparently was not a strict astronomical term during the time of development of mythology. All of the myths using these terms indicate the words are associated with some characteristics similar to the polar plasma. They do not, however, all directly indicate a location at a pole. The phrase may be interpreted as such, but is not definitely that location. For example, the "navel" or "center" of the Earth or sea or sky could mean a pole, but not necessarily.

The following is to provide a flavor of the correlations and is not an exhaustive comparison.

A Scandinavian myth describes the tree Yggdrasil. "Yggdrasil, the mighty ash tree, grew at the center of all, rooted in all the realms from the darkest to the lightest, from the lowest to the highest" [Caldecott, p. 159]. The sacred tree is often at the center of a garden. Persphone was the daughter of Demeter, Greek Goddess of the Bountiful Harvest. Hades tempted her with a pomegranate tree that was in the 'midst' of a black and blighted garden. A tree was in the center of The Garden of Eden and had the snake symbols and orb-like symbol of an apple.

"The birch tree is the Cosmic Tree of shamanism, and the shaman ascends the seven or nine notches of the tree trunk or birch pole, symbolizing the ascent through the planetary spheres of the Supreme

Spirit" [Caldecott, p. 155]. Although the number of distinct levels varies from about three to ten, "Generally, in an intense electrical discharge in the multimegavolt, multimegaampere range, as would be measured in an intense aurora, nine distinct pinches that are spheroidal in shape are formed" [Peratt, p. 1195]. This fits well with the often cited seven or nine levels of or to heaven.

Brown indicated that Hindu scriptures have a similar description as the Lakota for the significance of the World Tree. "The World Tree in which the trunk which is also the sun pillar, sacrificial post, and axis mundi, rising from the altar at the naval of the earth, penetrates the world door and branches out above the roof of the world" [Brown, J.].

Black Elk described the Sacred Cottonwood Tree and the Sun Dance of the North American Sioux. He said, "... each of the posts around the lodge represents some particular object of creation, and the one tree at the center, upon which the twenty-eight poles rest, is THE GREAT SPIRIT, who is the center of everything" [Caldecott, p. 202]. This is similar to the importance of a tree at the center, but another important item with respect to the plasma is the number twenty-eight.

Section XVII of Peratt's article is titled »Petroglyphs Associated With The Circular Aurora Plasma«. In part B of that section, he describes "Records From Antiquity With 56- and 28-Fold Symmetry." A number of very early symmetrical petroglyphs contain one of those numbers of dots. Peratt presents overlays of petroglyphs with the plasma dots and monuments constructed later. [Peratt, p. 1210] He has also correlates various art objects with the same pattern.

Peratt observed that laboratory discharges often begin with 56 Birkeland currents (filaments) equally spaced around the periphery of a cylinder. With time, the filaments pair up and combine into 28 filaments. If paring continues, the discharge will end with 4 filaments that pinch plasma to the center.

Comet Venus

The ancients described Venus, or the equivalent plasmoid, as often having a comet-like appearance. A number of ancient symbols for Venus have comet features. From the side, a comet has a general appearance such as depicted in figure 12. The view from being closer reveals more detail in the structure and activity of the streamers. In the following, mainly the plasma tails will be considered.

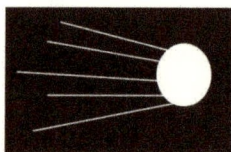

Figure 12 Depiction of comet like plasma streamers.

Nearly everywhere on Earth, ancient societies said that Venus and comets had some similar characteristics. Today Venus has almost none of those attributes visible. Those comet characteristics include a visible long flowing tail and an orbit considerably unlike that of the other planets. (Although Venus has "comet-like" plasma interaction with the Solar Wind [Wallis], that interaction is not currently visible to the eye from Earth.)

The ancients apparently saw things we do not see. Therefore, the most likely explanations, assuming that ancients were taking data and not imagining things, are that

1) Venus mythology did not originate with the behavior of Venus but was associated with Venus because of comet activity occurring near Venus, or that

2) Venus, within the time of people, had some comet-like characteristics. These comet characteristics would be ones visible from the Earth by the unaided eye.

The ancients did not define a comet as modern science does. The characteristics the ancients attributed to both Venus and comets include: long flowing hair, snake-like appearance, dragon-like appearance, and sometimes-disheveled hair. In addition, both were called tailed stars, torch stars, smoking stars, and bearded stars. Comets were also called "circling star", "torch", and "Angel of the Lord" [Fuhr, 1982, p. 48].

The angel of the Lord apparently was destructive. Second Kings 19:35, of the King James Version of the Bible says, "And it came to pass that night, that the angel of the LORD went out, and smote in the camp of the Assyrians an hundred fourscore and five thousand: and when they arose early in the morning, behold, they were all dead corpses." You could see why the ancients would fear an object in the sky that appeared to do that.

Although a number of these characteristics would not seem strange being applied to comets, these characteristics do not fit the current Venus. Both Venus and comets were also associated with war, major disruptions, and long periods of darkness. Velikovsky may have been the first to note recently that the ancients claimed most of these similarities for Venus and comets and that the *comets* caused problems on the Earth [Velikovsky, 1950, p. 163ff]. Interestingly, Sagan and Druyan, in *Comet,* later said that nearly all ancients attributed a number of bad characteristics to comets [Cochrane, 2001, p. 130]. A number of other investigators have reached this same conclusion. This association of Venus and comets does not make sense from what is seen in the sky today. It does make sense within some of the detailed models found elsewhere that are beyond the scope of this article.

Comets created so much fear that the images of comets were incorporated into many ceremonies. Some of those comet images are still associated with activities of modern people. For example, numerous churches have steeples that look like comets. In some cases, the entire front of a small church looks like a comet. Long flowing trains used in weddings have a very distinct comet appearance.

In 1950, astronomers assumed that Venus was very much like Earth. From the ancient descriptions of the comet-like appearance and activities of Venus, Velikovsky concluded that Venus was nothing like Earth. He was correct. Details are presented later. This is one of the areas where he was correct in noting that Venus should not have Earth-like characteristics, but the detailed model of why is still debated. It may be that Venus is a relatively young planet or that a large comet collided with Venus and created the conditions found there. The comet could have had an interaction with Earth before the collision with Venus and the destructive attributes of the comet were transferred to the planet Venus. There may be other possibilities. That question is for those interested in developing detailed models of the recent history of the Solar System, which is beyond the scope of this article.

Natural Phenomena Inspired Petroglyphs

The previous information provided physical support for point A (The ancient sky inspired prehistoric rock art) and point B (Early myths, first oral and later written, mimic images and activities seen in the ancient sky). Both of these suggest that the ancient sky was different.

To reiterate, Velikovsky's top level concepts were:

1. The appearance of the sky underwent noticeable changes within the time of people.
2. The images and activities in the ancient sky inspired mythology.
3. Electromagnetic fields played a significant part in the appearance of the Solar System to the ancients.
4. Catastrophes of a global nature impacted at least the environment on the Earth and possibly some geological structures.
5. A detailed model of the recent history of the Solar System can be enhanced using data from mythology.

The support provided for points A and B demonstrate that Velikovsky was right about his top level concepts 1) and 2). The support provided was not taken from Velikovsky's works; therefore, the discussion no longer relies only on Velikovsky's extensive publications. The support also had a strong foundation in physics and the scientific method; therefore, the discussion does not rely only on interpretation of written data the ancients recorded.

Points A and B also strongly suggest Velikovsky's ideas with respect to points 3) and 4) are correct. The following section provides support for the concept that something happened within the history of the Solar System that does not fit with the 1950 accepted concept of the origin of the Solar System. That concept is basically the concept still used by many astronomers.

As noted earlier, this article does not cover 5). The data combined with support for 1), 2), 3), and 4), however, does strongly suggest that Velikovsky's concept that a model can be constructed is also highly likely, although his detailed model may have flaws.

Unexpected Solar System

Additional support showing that the ancient sky was different comes from comparing what was expected to be found in the Solar System with two alternate concepts.

- The generally accepted gravity based concept that says nothing major has changed in the Solar System since its origin and that gravity is the only significant force that ever acted on the bodies in the Solar System. This will be referred to as the *old concept*.
- Velikovsky's combined plasma (electromagnetic)-gravity-historical based concept that indicates something has changed in the Solar System within the last 50,000 years and that plasma played an important part in the activity. This will be referred to as the *new*[1] *concept*.

Researchers have compared both concept models to what space probes found in the Solar System. Since 1950, proponents of the old concept have said that numerous results of the space age are "surprising" or "unexpected." Many of those same results were not surprising to proponents of the new concept and fit nicely within the new concept. Some of the results were even anticipated by Velikovsky. A number of Velikovsky's "advance claims" will be described later.

This section deals with the discoveries of the space age that were unexpected by the *old concept* and difficult to explain by that concept. Some of the unexpected finds are either not surprising based on plasma science or were anticipated by plasma scientists. In science, if the results of an experiment do not fit what you thought based on theory,

---

[1] New is relative in that Velikovsky introduced the concept over fifty years ago.

the theory is often considered wrong. That has not been the case with the *old concept*. It seems that very little of the data fits what was anticipated, but the theory is still considered correct.

In the early part of the twentieth century, scientists developed a theory about the origin of the Solar System by observing what they could then see from Earth and assuming that everything they saw was nearly the way it had been for billions of years. You must admit that the approach is reasonable for a first approximation.

The developers of that theory did ignore one source of data. That source was historical observations by the ancients. The basis for ignoring that data was that the ancients described activities that appeared so outlandish that they could not have occurred. This attitude is now changing, but that attitude certainly influenced the ideas in 1950.

Plasma science at the time was almost unknown even among many scientists in other fields, so plasma effects were not considered. It is partially understandable why they did not consider that data. The scientists in 1950 also did not have access to data from on-site measurements outside Earth. They thought they knew what they would find and thought what they would find would not change any opinions.

So the generally accepted theory in 1950 was developed assuming that no significant changes had occurred in the Solar System since its origin and that the only major influence during all of the Solar System activities was gravity. That theory was then used to make a number of predictions about what would be found in the Solar System when space probes became available. That theory was also used to ridicule any theory that indicated the Solar System origin and activities were not as straightforward as indicated by the generally accepted theory.

The exotic models and some of the less exotic models of the ancient sky indicate that pre-historic people saw unusual activity in the ancient sky. Some of that activity involved what later people identified as planets. As noted, the activity may have been from near-earth plasma and the plasma characteristics may have been transferred to the planets by later people who did not see the unusual activity. Transference appeared to have happened with respect to the constellations.

Some of the unusual activity may have been from comets. Characteristics and stories about those comets may have also been transferred to the planets by later people who did not see the unusual activity. It is also possible that multiple ancient comets had near encounters and even collisions with visible planets. These events, visible to some extent from Earth, could have created some of the features found in the Solar System that were unexpected in 1950.

Therefore, it is interesting to compare what the accepted 1950 theory predicted to what space probes found. We shall see the space age discoveries were often announced using the words "surprising" or "unexpected" or similar exclamations of astonishment. The results were strikingly more in line with what would be expected based on Velikovsky's view of the Solar System than on the generally accepted view of 1950.

In the mid-nineteenth century, an Italian astronomer named Giovanni Schiaparelli, observed Mercury and concluded that Mercury always keeps one side facing the Sun, much as our Moon perpetually presents only one face to Earth. The suggested explanation was the same as for the Moon. The tidal bulge raised in Mercury by the Sun supposedly had modified the planet's rotation rate until the bulge always pointed directly at the Sun. Schiaparelli's observations and the later observations by astronomers who saw what they wanted to see were combined with a plausible physical explanation. That was enough to convince most astronomers that Mercury rotated synchronously with its revolution about the Sun (i.e., once every 88 Earth days). In 1965, astronomers made radar observations of Mercury and discovered that the rate was not 88 days but 59 days.

In 1951, Arthur C. Clarke published *The Exploration of Space*. In it, he said, "Although we do not know the composition and pressure of the Venusian atmosphere at the surface of the planet, it is certainly at least as dense as Earth's, but probably not so compressed that it would be dangerous to human life" [Clarke p. 143]. The pressure of Venus' atmosphere at the surface was later shown to be as high as the pressure one kilometer deep in the ocean on the Earth.

In 1962, Sir Patrick Moore wrote *The Planets*. In it, he said, "Probably the magnetic field of Venus is appreciably stronger than that of our own world, so that electrical phenomena there are only too likely" [Moore p. 52]. More recent results indicate that Venus has no magnetic field, but electrical phenomena, including two distinct x-ray producing layers in the atmosphere, are more abundant than expected. Moore also said, "D. H. Menzel and F. L. Whipple hold the view that the clouds are simply H_2O, and that the surface of Venus is almost entirely covered with water" [Moore p. 54]. Later results indicate that the clouds are not water and the surface temperature of Venus is hot enough to melt lead.

In 1962, Moore said, "We do not believe that other intelligent beings exist in the Solar System, but it is likely that there is plenty of 'vegetation' on Mars, and there may be primitive marine organisms on Venus" [Moore p. 65]. In 1963, on a television program titled *The Clouds of Venus,* Carl Sagan said, "... measurements show temperature at the surface of Venus could support life similar to that on Earth." Very soon after that program aired, data showed that Venus is considerably hotter than most investigators had previously believed. Venus' surface is actually hotter than Mercury's surface despite Venus being nearly twice as far from the Sun as is Mercury.

The 1950s idea that all the planets formed about the same time in the same manner and that nothing significant has interfered with this arrangement makes it seem reasonable that all the planets should rotate in the same direction and maybe even have similar tilt in their axes of rotation. Therefore, one of the bigger surprises since 1950 was the discovery that Venus spins the opposite direction of what was expected. That means that Venus spins backwards. In addition, early researchers thought that the tilt of the axis of Venus was around 23 degrees, or near that of the tilt to the axis of the Earth. Another surprise was that the tilt of the axis of Venus is around zero degrees.

Mark Perew is a freelance writer, a member of the National Association of Science Writers and a JPL Solar System Ambassador. On January 19, 2001, he placed an article on the *Universe Today* web site. In the article, he noted some unexpected results from analysis of data from Venus. One of these results was evidence of atomic oxygen in the atmosphere of Venus. The work was performed by astronomers from SRI International in Menlo Park, California, and the Lowell Observatory in Flagstaff, Arizona. "This comes as a major surprise" because until then, they had detected only molecular oxygen, O_2 and ozone. Perew said, "For the second day in a row, astronomers and astrophysicists have released new results which diametrically contradict previous understanding of Earth's nearest neighbor. *These results severely question how well we understand a planet with such stark differences, yet so close at hand and so similar in size and mass.*"

If the planet Venus were involved in the activity seen by the ancients instead of a comet that later had its characteristics associated with

Venus, it would not be surprising to find that Venus has features that are not exactly what would be expected by the generally accepted theory.

Venus is unexpectedly radically different from Earth. Venus has an unexpectedly high surface temperature that can approach 758 K (about 485 °C or 900 °F). The atmospheric pressure is 90 times greater than that of the Earth, and is about the same as the pressure at a depth of 1 km in Earth's oceans. Gravity on Venus is similar to that of Earth but the mass of the atmosphere would crush a person. The surface is mountainous and has a number of volcanoes and some are higher than Mt. Everest. Venus rotates in the opposite direction from Earth and very slowly. That was definitely not expected. The rotation rate of the planet is about 244 days, but the upper atmosphere rotation period is about four days. The rotation rate of Venus is close to a resonant spin-orbit interaction with the Earth. The same side of Venus always faces Earth when the Earth and Venus are closest together. That was not expected.

In late 1978, Pioneer probes discovered unexpectedly large quantities of the isotope argon-36. Argon-36 is supposed to be an argon isotope formed when the solar system was born. Argon-36 is radioactive so most of the original supply of that isotope should have disintegrated over the 4-billion-year history of the solar system. That is the case for the atmospheres of Earth and Mars, which have significantly smaller quantities of argon-36 than Venus. That corresponds with the low crater count on the surface. One explanation might be that the planet is younger than some others. The commonly accepted explanation for such few craters is that the surface must be refreshed often.

It was discovered after 1950 that Venus has a plasma tail that extends nearly to Earth. If Peratt is correct that Earth's ancient magnetosphere was considerably more active in the past and produced extensive visible effects not seen today, then it is reasonable to assume also that the plasma tail of Venus may also have been more visible at the time. I am not suggesting a model about the recent history of the Solar System, but it seems reasonable that one or more models may consider that possibility.

Venus was often described as a comet. Part of the 1950s argument about why the ancients must have been delusional was the accepted scientific opinion about the nature of comets. As previously noted, it does not really matter what the modern scientific definition is, the ancients called something in the sky with a tail a comet. If Venus looked like that, to the ancients Venus was a comet. It is interesting, however, to see if there were any surprises after 1950 about the nature of comets.

A comet is often thought of as a ball of frozen rock and ice or an assembly of frozen gases and dust orbiting the sun. Modern observations do not support that model [Scott, 2006]. Some investigators have called this the dirty snowball model. Some of the material vaporizes on nearing the Sun to produce a long veil-like luminous tail. Comet dust forms a cloud of debris that trails the comet in its orbit around the sun.

Some theorists speculated that dusty gas surrounding the rapidly vaporizing core might scatter a small number of high-energy photons from the Sun, producing a faint x-ray halo.

In 1996, astronomers using ROSAT satellite images were shocked by what they saw from Hyakutake. They found a crescent-shaped region of x-ray emission around the comet 1000 times more intense than anyone had predicted. Dr. Michael J. Mumma of NASA's Goddard Space Flight Center wrote, "We had no clear expectation that comets [would] shine in X-rays." "Now we have our work cut out for us explaining these data, but that's the kind of problem you love to have."

Later, x-rays were found around Comet LINEAR. Observations of Comet LINEAR revealed a strong x-ray signal from oxygen and nitrogen atoms that had lost most of their electrons. Stripping away as many as six electrons takes a lot of energy. This can only happen in a high-energy environment where violent collisions or strong radiation disrupts the atom. This is a plasma state.

Scientists believe that the ions around Comet LINEAR were carried there from the Sun's corona by fast-moving solar winds. Positively charged ions like oxygen missing six electrons make up about one percent of this solar wind. When the ions go past a comet, the strong positive charge of the ion attracts negatively charged electrons from atoms and molecules associated with the comet. The process of the electrons from the neutral atoms attaching to the solar wind ions would emit x-rays.

NASA launched the Chandra X-ray Observatory in 1999. Chandra images of Comet LINEAR revealed an x-ray glow surrounding the Sun-facing side of its nucleus. The cold nucleus itself was invisible at x-ray wavelengths, but the "gas" (i.e. plasma) around it was alive with variable x-ray emission.

This seemingly incongruous result – energetic x-rays coming from the vicinity of a cosmic snowball – did not amaze the researchers who were studying Comet LINEAR. They had already been amazed a few years earlier by Comet Hyakutake.

Comets' ion tails were generally thought of as pointing almost straight away from the Sun. The magnetometer data from Ulysses as it approached a comet revealed that the tail was definitely not pointing away from the sun; it was traveling almost sideways.

A few weeks before Ulysses' comet tail crossing, some observers reported tail lengths for Hyakutake that were "much longer than possible if comet tails are assumed to be straight, and pointing away from the Sun," says Jones. "The Ulysses magnetic field measurements show that these assumptions aren't true."

As previously noted, a number of investigators have begun to analyze comet tails as plasmas. The thinking now is that a comet may have a dusty tail and a plasma tail. Plasmas are known to emit x-rays under certain conditions. The shock about the intensity of the x-rays may have been less had the plasma effect been analyzed more closely instead of just considering dust scattering high-energy photons from the Sun.

Mars did not fit what was expected in 1950

Information by 1962 had already changed some 1950 ideas about Mars. Moore noted, "The old idea of Mars as a frozen world seems to be very wide off the mark" [Moore p. 82]. In some areas, the summer temperature may be as high as seventy degrees Fahrenheit. That same year Moore said that the atmosphere of Mars had 98.5 percent nitrogen and 0.25 percent carbon dioxide [Moore p. 90]. Later probe measurements indicated only 3 percent nitrogen and 95 percent carbon dioxide. Then it was 93 percent carbon dioxide, 2.7 percent nitrogen, and 1.6 percent Argon.

Also, in 1962, it was believed that there were no large hills on Mars [Moore p. 89]. Mariner 9 was launched 1971. Mariner 9 orbited Mars and photographed 100 percent of the planet's surface. "It uncovers many unexpected findings, like huge volcanoes, a 3,000 mile-long canyon, and ancient river beds." One volcano on Mars is now thought to be the largest volcano in the Solar System. This does not fit well at all with the generally accepted model of the origin of the Solar System. The volcano is called Olympus Mons and is twenty-four kilometers high (over seventy-five thousand feet). Mount Everest is slightly less than nine kilometers high.

In 1998, Mars Global Surveyor gravitational and magnetic field experiments revealed unexpected local phenomena "that have changed our interpretation of the planet's subsurface structure," according to Mars Global Surveyor scientists.

Analysis of results from NASA's Mars Global Surveyor led researchers to conclude that Mars had a magnetic field early in its history. In the ancient crust of the southern hemisphere there are stripes of magnetized crust of alternating polarity. These 100 km wide stripes run roughly parallel for 2000 km. The stripes alternate in polarity. The north magnetic pole of one points up from the surface and the north magnetic pole of the next points down into the surface. Geologists did not expect the strength and structure of the magnetism. The field strength seemed to be more than ten times what was expected. Henri Reme at the Jet Propulsion Laboratory in Pasadena, California said, "the surprise was fantastic."

Similar stripes were previously discovered on the Earth's seafloor. These stripes were fundamental in gaining acceptance for the theory of plate tectonics in the 1960s. Geologists now wonder if the stripes on Mars mean that plate tectonics occurred on Mars. However, the Martian stripes are wider, much more strongly magnetized than those on Earth, and do not appear to spread out from a central spreading zone.

In the Indiana Dunes National Lakeshore, Mt. Baldy is a coastal blowout dune that is currently advancing over a forest. What is called the slip face is gradually burying tree trunks. This is typical activity for dunes that are not cemented.

A picture from the Mars Global Surveyor, Mars Orbiter Camera, Release number MOC2-410, is one of thousands of images of what are called sand dunes on Mars [MSSS]. Researchers say that some dunes appear cemented. This means that the sand is not loose. There are also no craters. That indicates the dunes are rather young.

Cemented dunes leave steep-sided chutes on the slip face slope. Chutes are inclined troughs or channels. Some of these dunes are grooved indicating that they have been cemented and then eroded by wind. Some dunes have deep scars formed on the slip face slopes by avalanches of sand. The picture mentioned depicts more than a dozen examples.

The caption by NASA said that the pictures indicate that many dunes on Mars are cemented and inactive in the current environment on Mars. However, they note that these dunes were active sometime in the not-too-distant past and that that suggests the climate of Mars may have changed in recent times.

A probe to Mars found a "strange, unexpected phenomenon," over Mars' North Polar Region. This was an intense polar vortex that causes Mars' atmosphere to be less dense than predicted for that area. This is the inverse of the Venus atmospheric pressure surprise in that at least part of the atmosphere of Mars is thinner than expected.

At least one unexpected item found on Mars that fits well with the plasma concepts about the Solar System can be reproduced in the laboratory. In 2004, a Mars rover photographed small gray spherules dubbed blueberries. Scientists determined that the spherules were composed of hematite and some scientists assumed that the spherules were formed by water. Later experiments determined that similar spherules could be produced in a plasma laboratory without water. The experiments were described at a 2005 American Physical Society meeting [Ransom 2005].

Mars currently has two moons – Phobos and Deimos. The moons have nearly circular orbits and have nearly equatorial orbits. It is difficult to explain those orbits using the accepted idea of the origin of the solar system. In 2002, Professor S. F. Singer said, "Nobody has been able to explain the origin of Phobos and Deimos" [David, 7/03]. He said that previous models violate the laws of physics or do not account for the data.

At the 6th International Conference on Mars, Singer suggested that the problems with previous models could be overcome by saying that the moons are debris from a catastrophic demise of a larger moon that Mars captured soon after the formation of Mars. He said his theory predicts that the moons have similar composition, but current data does not indicate that the moons have similar composition. Singer said that core samples into the moons would be needed to test his theory.

That the current data does not fit his theory appears not to be a deterrent to people who want to consider the theory.

The information about the moons of Mars may not be a great surprise as is other data in this chapter. However, the information is significant with respect to the attitude in 1950. Then astronomers told people who questioned the accepted ideas that the orbits of the planets and moons were already explained so other ideas could not be correct. Also, the accepted idea was that motions of the planets and their moons had existed since the system began. Now we know the model astronomers claimed to be extremely accurate did not really explain as much as astronomers advertised. Therefore, claiming that other models were wrong because the accepted model must be correct was unfounded.

Another item mentioned at the conference was that astronomers do not expect Phobos to last more than a few million years. If that is the case, how many moons may have been around a few million years ago that are not here now? How many disappeared because of collisions with their primary body? Did any of those collisions happen within the time of people?

In 1950, astronomers told the public that nothing like that happened and the planets and their moons were stable. Now we are told that that is not the case. The point is not whether it is true that Phobos may collide with Mars in a few million years or that some other body collided with another planet in the geologically recent past. The point is that the assumed stability of the Solar System could not be used in 1950 and cannot be used today as proof that Velikovsky's ideas are wrong just because those ideas include the possibility that there were recent changes in the Solar System.

Saturn

Another set of examples of the unexpected are from Saturn and its moons.

A big surprise about Saturn was the strange aspects of the rings. Braids, kinks, and spokes were both unexpected and difficult to explain by gravity. The features are not that difficult to explain by plasma.

Morehead Planetarium published information about results from Pioneer and Voyager 1 and 2. The planetarium page said that the rings were a great surprise. They expected the rings to be broad and featureless. Instead, the rings looked like the groves in a twentieth century sound recording mechanism called a phonograph record. The rings were composed of about a thousand concentric circles. The gaps were expected to be empty, but they were also filled with a series of ringlets. They said that the "most astonishing" was that the thin F ring consisted of several streams of particles, "looped and braided about each other in apparent defiance of normal laws of physics." Defiance may be true if you only consider gravitational physics; however, it fits well with plasma physics.

Earthlink also described another unexpected feature in the B ring. A series of dark radial spokes on the B ring circled Saturn "for about one ring orbit period and then disappeared." The spokes appeared to be fine dust held in place by electrostatic forces. As the electric field disappeared, so did the spokes.

In 2003, x-rays were found being emitted by Saturn. The distribution was unexpected for the theory that the x-rays were scattered solar x-rays. On March 8, 2004, the space.com staff quoted Ness of the University of Hamburg in Germany as saying, "It's a puzzle, since the intensity of Saturn's x-rays requires that Saturn reflects x-rays fifty times more efficiently than the Moon." The staff also noted that the weak radiation from the South Polar Region was also a puzzle.

In 2004, the Cassini probe provided data that disclosed an unexpected radiation belt around Saturn. Donald Mitchell, of Johns Hopkins University, who is an instrument scientist for the imager, said, "It came as a huge surprise to us" [Groshong].

Titan is a moon of Saturn. Scientists thought Titan's atmosphere is similar to Earth's early atmosphere. The expectation was that Titan could help scientists determine aspects of early terrestrial biology, assuming that the atmospheric chemistry was an important factor. "Well, you can forget that, says Bruce Jakosky, of the University of Colorado. 'The reasons we originally looked to Titan are long gone. The putative reducing atmosphere of the early Earth – one that was oxygen poor and hydrogen rich – is no longer in fashion.' Titan is its own world, and not a time capsule of our own." [Shostak]

One of the innermost moons of Saturn is called Mimas. One of the craters, named Herschel, is surprisingly large in comparison to the size of the moon. Mimas does not have uniform crater sizes or distribution. The larger craters found elsewhere on Mimas are generally not found in the south-polar region. Investigators assumed that the larger craters were there at one time and that some process removed the larger craters from these areas.

Enceladus, another of the innermost moons of Saturn, is about 500 kilometers across. It is slightly larger than Mimas. Enceladus has a smooth, bright surface that reflects almost 100 percent of the sunlight that strikes it. Images of Enceladus depict at least five different types of terrain. In some locations there are craters no larger than 35 km in diameter. Other areas show regions with no craters at all. That is taken as an indication of major resurfacing events in the geologically recent past. The assumption is not necessary when considering plasma science. Images of Enceladus also depicted huge and unexpected faults.

A number of these features were unexpected and difficult to explain with the generally accepted theory in 1950. The features are not so difficult to explain assuming a changing plasma Solar System.

Planets other than Saturn, Venus and Mars were involved in the activities described by the ancients. It is interesting that unexpected results are found throughout the Solar System. A few examples are provided here.

Jupiter was also a major player in the deity planet world

In the early 1950's, the generally accepted idea was that Jupiter was an inactive dead planetary body. Hess and Mead said that, before 1965, most models of Jupiter and Saturn were based on the assumption that those were "completely cold planets." [Hess, 1965] This idea indicated that looking for radio noise on Jupiter would be a waste of time. However, a few years after 1950, investigators found radio noise. "But for a fortunate accident, nothing might have been known of Jupiter's radio flashes" [Smith, 1960]. It was a fortunate *accident* only because astronomers refused to take Velikovsky's suggestion and look for radio noise being emitted from Jupiter.

In 1996, it was noted that, "... Jupiter's atmosphere is just as turbulent and stormy as that of a bona fide star" [*Science News,* Vol. 150, 1996, p. 133]. In addition, there was Jupiter probe data "suggesting that heat escaping from deep within the planet, rather than sunlight striking Jupiter's topmost layers, drives the circulation," [*Science News,* Vol. 149, 1/27/1996, p. 55]. This heat could be caused from gravitational collapse, but this article leaves the impression that this heat was not initially considered to be the cause of the turbulent atmosphere.

An "unexpected discovery" from Voyager was rings around Jupiter. The ring particles appear to extend nearly all the way down to Jupiter. One suggestion was that "the ring particles are a source of oxygen that is related to the carbon monoxide that was *unexpectedly* found in the Jovian atmosphere." [Italics added]

In 1950, astronomers did not consider that Jupiter had rings. In 1976, Pioneer 10 acquired information about particles near Jupiter. Astronomers interpreted the data as suggesting that extremely low-density rings around Jupiter were "unlikely." S. F. Singer and J. E. Stanley of the University of Virginia in Charlottesville said, "We see no evidence for particles in permanent Jovicentric orbits" [Singer]. In 1997, Voyager spacecraft obtained pictures of the rings around Jupiter. Later, the Galileo probe provided data confirming that there were tenuous rings around Jupiter.

Dr. David Whitehouse is the *BBC News Online* science editor. On July 17, 2001, he wrote an article entitled *Jupiter's Clouds Puzzle Experts.* In the article, he quoted Dr. Carolyn Porco of the Southwest Research Institute in Boulder, Colorado. She said, "This is the first movie ever made of the motions of Jupiter's clouds near the poles and it seems to indicate that one notion concerning the nature of the circulation on Jupiter is incomplete at best, and possibly wrong."

In 2004, scientists from the Los Alamos National Laboratory said that Jupiter and Saturn *formed in completely different ways.* Part of the information used in the analysis was that certain heavy metals were concentrated in the core of Saturn but the same metals were diffused in Jupiter [Dankeskoild].

Not only is the idea that Jupiter and Saturn being formed in completely different ways not surprising to Velikovsky's model, being formed differently would be expected.

The Galileo probe provided results that were interpreted to indicate a hole in Jupiter's magnetic field. Researchers expected the magnetic field to increase continuously as the probe approached Jupiter. However, suddenly the magnetic field strength dropped about thirty percent. Dr. Margaret Kivelson of the University of California at Los Angeles leads Galileo's magnetic fields investigation team. She said, "It's an astonishing result and completely unexpected." One interpretation is that Io, a moon of Jupiter, has its own magnetic field and somehow causes the hole, but exactly how is not clear" [Murrill].

After examining data from the Voyager probe, researchers were very surprised to see that Io's surface is radically different from any other body in the Solar System. Instead of craters, the images depicted hundreds of volcanic calderas, and some of the volcanoes are active. There are very few, if any, impact craters on Io. Researchers concluded that the surface is very young and that any impact craters have been covered because of the volcanic activity. Another surprise about Io was that its active sulfurous volcanoes send dust particles out as far as 180 million miles.

The European Space Agency and NASA launched the space probe Ulysses in 1990. Ulysses approached Jupiter in 1992 and detected what was considered to be volcanic dust traveling at excessively high speed. The particles were also accelerating away from Io, which is not what you expect from only the influence of gravity. This action is reasonable in plasma. Harold Krueger of the Max Planck Institute in Heidelberg said, "What a surprise ... We expected to encounter dust, but nothing like this." In 2004, Ulysses again approached Jupiter. There was still dust from what were still thought to be volcanoes, but "The dust was shooting in the wrong direction" [NASA 2004].

Space probes also discovered that some volcanoes on Io move. One moved over forty miles in about sixteen years. Since volcanoes do not move, scientists decided that only the plume moved. Forty miles in sixteen years is still unusual. The probes also discovered that the ejected material shoots up but does not fall onto the surface over an area similar to that produced by a volcano. The material falls onto a circumferential ring. A moving volcano, material accelerating away from the plume in a manner not expected by gravity, and material distributed in a ring are characteristics that can be more easily explained by plasmas than by volcanoes and gravity.

Ganymede, another moon of Jupiter, is the only known planetary satellite with its own magnetic field, a trait that surprised planetary geologists. Richard Stenger, a CNN writer, quoted Torrence Johnson, a NASA scientist at the Jet Propulsion Laboratory in Pasadena, California, as saying, "How did it get so hot that liquid iron in its core moves around enough to make a magnetic field? Either something's wrong with our theory or our understanding of Ganymede's history." In an interview with Jeffrey Kaye on KCET- Los Angeles, Johnson said, "We really hadn't expected that satellite or moon to have a magnetic field. It's cold, made out of ice mostly with rock in its center, and yet, when we flew by, two of our instruments clearly saw an indication that it had a magnetic field."

Data from Galileo about Ganymede caused some to "turn our previous thinking upside down" [*Science News,* Vol. 150, July 20, 1996, p. 37]. There were surprises from other probe data. Data from the "... mass spectrometer indicate that several elements, including carbon, oxygen, and sulfur, have abundances closer to solar values than previously thought. This suggests that scientists don't fully understand how the planets evolved, Owen says" [*Science News,* Vol. 149, 1/27/ 1996, p. 55]. From previous data, Professor J. H. Hoffman said, "It sure means that we've got to rethink the whole formation theories of the inner planets of the Solar System" [*The Dallas Morning News,* 12/11/1979].

Dr. David Whitehouse, the *BBC News Online* science editor mentioned earlier, wrote an article about another moon of Jupiter, Amalthea, on December 10, 2002, not long after the spacecraft Galileo provided information about it. He quoted Dr. John Anderson of the Jet Propulsion Laboratory (JPL) as saying, "The density is unexpectedly low," and, "Amalthea is apparently a loosely packed pile of rubble."

Dr. Whitehouse also noted, "scientists are surprised" about the density. These measurements indicate that Amalthea's density is so low that even the solid parts of Amalthea are apparently less dense than Io, mentioned above, which is a larger moon of Jupiter and orbits about twice as far from Jupiter as does Amalthea. However, the generally accepted model for the formation of Jupiter's moons suggests moons closer to the planet would be made of denser material than those farther out. This anomaly was called "puzzling."

Uranus and Neptune

Uranus has rings. It was a surprise when astronomers found the rings in 1977.

Voyager 1 and Voyager 2 were launched in 1977. They initially had a two-planet mission to fly by Jupiter and then Saturn. With great technical skill, engineers used remote control reprogramming to endow the Voyagers with greater capabilities than they possessed when they left the Earth. This stretched their five-year lifetimes to over twelve. This allowed flybys of Uranus and Neptune and other planets.

One unexpected find was that Uranus had a magnetic axis that was highly skewed from the already known completely skewed rotational axis. The magnetic field is tilted almost sixty degrees with respect to the axis of rotation and offset from the planet's center. This gives Uranus an unusual magnetosphere. At the time that Voyager 2 approached Uranus, Uranus' South Pole was pointed almost directly at the Sun. This arrangement provides the polar region of Uranus with more energy input from the Sun than is received at its equatorial regions. However, Uranus is hotter at its equator than at its poles. The mechanism underlying this is unknown. Some researchers said, "It is probably generated by motion at relatively shallow depths within Uranus." That is not a very detailed theory.

Neptune's magnetic axis is skewed. "Neptune's magnetic field is, like Uranus', oddly oriented and probably generated by motions of conductive material (probably water) in its middle layers." Neptune's magnetic axis is angled at about forty-seven degrees to its rotation axis. When planetary scientists *found the odd tilt of the magnetic field on Uranus, they considered it an exception. Another exception on Neptune created some concern among planetary scientists about how planetary magnetic fields are generated [Kerr].*

Neptune has an internal heat source, like Jupiter and Saturn. Neptune radiates more than twice the energy it receives from the Sun.

In 1950, the assumption was that all planets formed about the same time in about the same manner. The assumption was used as proof that no changes had occurred in the solar system for billions of years. Using space age data from the planets reveals that the 1950 assumption was incorrect; however, some people still use that assumption as proof that the ancient sky could not have been different.

People at Cornell University mentioned an oddity about the asteroid Eros. They said that, because the gravity is so weak on Eros, you would expect that a large portion of the debris produced during collisions of space objects with Eros would have escaped. However, the surface of Eros has numerous rocks in the range of 30 to 100 meters across. Joseph Veverka mentioned a couple of possibilities. He said, "One is that we simply don't understand cratering events on small objects, and somehow the debris gets thrown out at very low speeds. Or the ejected material ends up in the same orbit as Eros, and over time the asteroid runs back into its own debris and gathers it up, which is equally bizarre. We simply don't understand this" [Veverka].

An area beyond Neptune contains multiple objects that have odd trajectories about the Sun and some have multiple satellite systems. "The problem is, current theories of the solar system's formation and evolution can't account for it all" [Britt].

Much of the data from space probes does not appear to make much sense with respect to what we currently believe about the recent history of the Solar System. The information is compatible with the ancient sky being different.

Bode Does Not Rule

An equation, called Bode's law in 1950, was used as an approximation of the distances of the planets from the Sun. The equation was not a law and was not discovered by Bode, it was discovered by Titius. The equation was later called the Titius-Bode Rule. The equation is $r = 0.4 + 0.3 \times 2^m$. The letter m starts at minus infinity and then takes values of 0, 1, 2, etc. As late as 1972, Schatzman mentioned that many cosmological theories assumed that the equation reflected conditions of the Solar System at the time of the formation of the planets billions of years ago [Schatzman]. Some scientists such as astronomer J. Q. Stewart in 1950 said the equation proved that Venus could not have ever been in a different orbit. Even as late at 1975, Sklower said she did not dispute the general theory; she questioned whether the order of the Solar System had ever changed [Sklower]. One of her reasons was that the Bode equation worked.

Today, few would consider the Titius-Bode Rule an accurate description of the original Solar System, although some may still use it to
claim that Velikovsky was wrong. Even those people abandon that
argument when I mention a variation of the equation. The Titius equation was developed to fit the current data. I wondered what would
happen if the data were different. By developing the equation for the
current system without the planet Venus, the equation is exactly like
the old equation except the 0.3 is replaced by 0.6. All the distances to
the planets are *exactly* as the Titius-Bode Rule, except the orbit of
Venus disappears [Ransom, 1980]. This of course does not mean that
Velikovsky was right, but it does demonstrate that the Titus-Bode Rule
cannot be used as support by people who claim he is wrong.

Earth Changes

The following information indicates that something unusual happened
in the time period being discussed. The something unusual can easily
fit with the events caused by the different ancient sky.

One example is from carbon dating. Figure 13 depicts what a typical
experimental curve would be expected to resemble if the atmosphere
were uniform for over five thousand years. Figure 14 depicts a fac-
simile of what was found experimentally. The figure was hand sketched
for illustration purposes only and does not represent Libby's exact
data.

Figure 13 Expected form of experimental curve if atmosphere uniform.

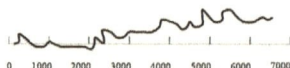

Figure 14 Experimental curve from Earth's changing atmosphere.

People interested in dating artifacts for historical purposes can successfully use experimental data similar to that depicted in figure 14. Those people are not necessarily interested in what caused the shape of the curve. Those people look at the curve and see a way to obtain useful carbon dates for artifacts. Creationists look at the curve and see proof of creation as described by the Bible. People interested in the different ancient sky look at the curve and see a *divergence from a uniform atmosphere at the time of the different ancient sky*. That is the observation of interest here. Nothing supernatural need be considered.

There are other indications that the Earth was influenced in an unusual way in the last 12,000 years. The following are a few examples that under further investigation may have other reasonable explanations, but could easily be considered as something that correlates with what the ancients seemed to have observed.

Dr. Geoffrey O. Seltzer, a geologist at Syracuse University, is interested in detailed investigation of the history of environmental and climatic change in the tropics during the time period of less than 20,000 years ago. He said that El Niños occur today once every two to eight years. However, his research indicates that between about 12,000 and 7,000 years ago strong El Niños occurred only about five times every hundred years.

An information release by The University of Washington in Seattle in January of 2003 contained information about the West Antarctic Ice Sheet. Research indicates that the ice sheet started melting 10,000 years ago and is likely to continue melting. The research was performed in part by Dr. John Stone, who is with the Quaternary Research Center and Department of Geological Sciences at The University of Washington.

It is often thought that a number of ancient civilizations disappeared because of common earthquakes. Ambraseys analyzed earthquakes and their effects in the past twenty-five centuries. He concluded that earthquakes alone couldn't account for the extreme changes or annihilation of ancient civilizations [Ambraseys]. In 2004 there were publications about at least four meteoric craters in southern Iraq attributed to impacts a few thousand years ago [Master]. Dr. Bill Napier said Northern Syria revealed a cataclysmic environmental event accompanied by destruction of mud-brick buildings caused by a "blast from the sky." He said that this also pointed to an encounter with a giant comet.

The Pleistocene to Holocene transition took place about 11,000 years ago. This change caused the extinction of a large number of animal species such as mammoths, mastodons and ground sloths. The change was dramatic. Dr. Russell Graham is an associate professor of geology and director of the Earth & Mineral Sciences Museum. At the February 19, 2006, meeting of the American Association for the Advancement of Science in St Louis, MO, in the US, he said, "The Pleistocene to Holocene transition occurred in about 40 years."

In *The New Catastrophism, The Importance of the Rare Event in Geological History*, geologist Derek Ager said, "Even within the brief life of mankind (with 99% of it in the 'Stone Age') there were great geological events that are not recorded in our histories" [Ager, p. xviii]. But the events *were* recorded. The recorded data is called myth and is ignored by some researches such as Ager.

In his book, it is clear that Ager believed most, if not all, processes now seen occurring on the Earth could explain all of the rare geological events. However, he also said, "For a century and a half the geological world has been dominated, one might even say brain-washed, by the gradualist uniformitarianism of Charles Lyell" [Ager, p. xi]. In addition, he said, "I must emphasize that I am concerned with the whole history of the Earth and its life and in particular with the dangerous doctrine of uniformitarianism" [Ager, p. xvi].

Review of Some of Velikovsky's Advance Claims

Velikovsky made advanced claims about what he expected would be found in the Solar System. He preferred not to call the advance claims predictions, because in the scientific would the word is often associated with a mathematical model, and in the non-scientific world the word is often associated with supposed psychic abilities. His claims were not based on either of those, but were based on observational data supplied by the ancients and logical conclusions drawn from those observations.

Velikovsky made specific advance claims about the Solar System based on his concepts about the recent history of the Solar System. The opposition in 1950 made specific advance claims about the Solar System based on their concept of the recent history of the Solar System. Velikovsky's claims were very often correct. The opposition's claims were very often not correct. As we discovered in the previous section, proponents of the accepted concept found the space probe results surprising or unexpected. To Velikovsky and proponents of his basic concept the results were not surprising. In addition, Velikovsky correctly anticipated what was found. The following details some of those advance claims.

A major advance claim was that events in the Solar System were more influenced by electromagnetic fields than was believed in 1950. This claim is directly tied to plasma science, which in turn directly supports the suggestion that the ancient sky was different.

In 1956, scientists accepted that Earth's magnetic field decreased with distance from the ground. Velikovsky said that the magnetic field above the ionosphere may be even stronger than at Earth's surface. Velikovsky submitted a memorandum to the U.S. National Committee for a planned International Geophysical Year through H. H. Hess, Chairman of the Department of Geology at Princeton University. He suggested that Earth's magnetic field would extend beyond the orbit of Earth's moon. One critic said that Velikovsky "invented" electromagnetic fields to explain events in the Solar System that could not happen. It is now known that what is called the magnetosphere is considerably more complex than thought in 1956, and it extends beyond the orbit of the moon.

Velikovsky said that Jupiter was an active planet and asked some astronomers to try to determine if radio noise could be found coming from Jupiter. They assured him that Jupiter was a cold dead planet and it would emit no radio noise. As late as 1964, Asimov, in what he intended to be a non-fiction book, wrote that Jupiter does not develop enough heat to warm its surface and that any warmth there is due to solar radiation [Asimov]. As noted earlier, by 1996, space probe data indicated that heat escaping from within the planet, not sunlight, drives the atmospheric circulation. We also saw that astronomers were surprised to discover radio noise from Jupiter years after Velikovsky asked astronomers to look for radio noise.

Before the first Moon landing, Velikovsky, through H. H. Hess, asked the people in charge of the Lunar Lander activities to measure the orientation of lunar rocks so the direction of the magnetic field could be determined. Velikovsky was assured that there would be no magnetic field, so there would be no need to measure the orientation of the rocks. Scientists were surprised that the rocks did have a magnetic field. This suggestion was not like Velikovsky's request to seek radio noise from Jupiter or test for the magnetosphere, which may have required a large unplanned expense. This suggestion would have been relatively inexpensive to implement. Lunar experts were so sure that remnant magnetic fields would not be found they published a paper several months before the lunar landing stating that no remnant magnetic field was expected. [Nature 221, 415,1969] Analysis of the direction was not possible because scientists were so sure of their basic concept that they would not even allow simple measurements at the time the rocks were collected.

Before 1940, some astronomers discussed "canals" on Mars. Many people liked to think of the canals as evidence of extinct or extant higher life forms on Mars. In 1974, Science magazine referred to those discussions as "an embarrassing epoch for American science ..." In 1950, Velikovsky reasoned that since ancient descriptions indicated that Mars was involved in destructive encounters with external debris, Mars would have been significantly damaged during the encounters. He said that anything on Mars that might appear to be canals would only be "a result of the play of geological forces that answered with rifts and cracks" on the surface of Mars. Sixteen years later, Opik said, "The canals may be cracks in the crust, radiating from the points of impact of colliding material" [Opik].

Olympus Mons is thought to be the largest volcano in the Solar System. It has a diameter of more than 500 km and a summit higher than 25 km above the surrounding plains. There are very few craters on its slopes, indicating that it is geologically very young. Velikovsky did not specifically claim that a large mountain would be found on Mars, but his description about what led to rifts and cracks is compatible with external forces that could reasonably create cracks that could lead to large volcanoes.

Velikovsky said that Venus would be considerably hotter than Earth and was possibly still molten. Twelve years later, Sagan and others were still saying that Venus was only slightly warmer than Earth and may even support life similar to that found on Earth. Soon after that, it was discovered that Velikovsky's description was correct.

Velikovsky also said that because of the ancient descriptions of the activities of Venus, he expected that Venus would have an anomalous rotation. This was confirmed when it was discovered that Venus spins backward. This completely contradicted the accepted concept about how the planets acquired their angular momentum. In addition, the spin rate of Venus was found to be about 243 Earth days instead of about one Earth day. The tilt of Venus was thought to be about that of Earth, about 23.45°, but the tilt of Venus is just a few degrees, not considering the sign of rotation. All of these easily fall under the scope of anomalous rotation. None were what astronomers of 1950 expected.

Although not an advance claim in astronomy, Velikovsky made a claim related to who said what when about images seen in the ancient sky. In 1950, he suggested that data from Mesoamerican cultures indicated that those cultures were much older than experts then accepted because of the timing of what it seemed that those cultures experienced. Opponents said Velikovsky described data from cultures that did not exist until the 4th to 8th centuries CE. Velikovsky said they must have been around much earlier than that. By 1967, Mesoamerican cultures were thought to have had major beginnings around 8000 BCE, 1500 BCE and 600 BCE [Flannery]. In 2005, researchers discovered the oldest known Mayan mural. This dated to 100 BCE. The mural depicts the establishment of order in the world by four Mayan deities and the life, death and resurrection of the maize god. Mayan legend says he crowned himself king of the world. These legends are similar to legends in other parts of the world and apparently were developed earlier. Whenever they were created, it is clear that Velikovsky was correct about Mesoamerican cultures existing before the current era.

Conclusion

Velikovsky made specific advance claims about the Solar System based on his concepts about the recent history of the Solar System. The opposition in 1950 made specific advance claims about the Solar System based on their concept of the recent history of the Solar System. Velikovsky's claims were very often correct. The opposition's claims were most often not correct. IF Velikovsky's claims had been often incorrect, the opposition would have said it proved that his basic concepts were incorrect. Since the opposition's claims WERE often incorrect, they should similarly conclude that their basic concepts were and are incorrect.

Plasma provides a physical foundation for the hypothesis that the ancient sky was different. The information about planets in myths implies that the ancient sky was different. It corresponds with the plasma information and suggests that the ancients were taking data instead of creating fictional stories. Velikovsky noted that the ancient data suggests that what would be found in the Solar System would not be what was expected in 1950. Space probe data supports that conclusion.

We have seen that plasmas can create many of the images seen by the ancients. It seems reasonable then to try to develop a comprehensive model of plasma effects and motions of various bodies in the sky that would explain the rest of the data. Over the last few centuries, a number of people including Velikovsky have tried just that. With what is known today, the job of developing a comprehensive model of the recent history of the Solar System should be easier.

In summary:

- There is a physical basis for concluding that the ancient sky was different
- There is a strong indication that plasma in the ancient sky inspired mythology
- It is essential to consider ancient myths and symbols as data the way Velikovsky did in order to understand the recent history of the Solar System.

References

Ager, Derek: *The New Catastrophism, The importance of the rare event in geological history* (Cambridge University Press, 1993)

Ambraseys, N. N.: *Nature* 232, 1971

Asimov, I.: *Adding a Dimension*, Avon Books, N.Y. 1964, p 193

Bednarik, Robert G.: *Rock Art Datings Withdrawn.*
http://www.cesmap.it/ifrao/res2.html

Bhattacharjee, Yudhijit: *Warning:* »Don't Let Your Elders Brainwash You«, *Science*, Vol.. 325, 29 August, 2009, p. 1060

Breuer, Hans: *Columbus Was Chinese: Discoveries of the Far East*, Translated by Salvator Attanasio, McGraw-Hill, 1972, ISBN: 0-07-073134-9, p. 229

Britt, Robert Roy, Senior Science Writer: »The Solar System Gets Crazier«, Space.com, posted: 19 December 2005

Brown, Joseph Epes: *The Sacred Pipe: Black Elk's Account of the Seven Rites of the Oglala Sioux*, University of Oklahoma Press, © 1989, p. 69

Brown, Vincent: *The Concept of the Djed Symbol*,
http://www.pyramidofman.com/Djed/

Budge, E. A. Wallis: *Egyptian Magic*, Dover Publications, New York, 1971

Caldecott, Moyra: *Myths of the Sacred Tree*, Destiny Books, 1993

Clarke, Arthur C.: *The Exploration of Space*, Harper & Brothers, 1951. Library of Congress number 52-5430.

Clube, Victor, and Napier, Bill: *The Cosmic Winter*, Basil Blackwell Ltd., Oxford, 1990

Cochrane, Ev: *Martian Metamorphoses: The Planet Mars in Ancient Myth and Religion*, Aeon Press, 1997, ISBN 0-9656229-8

Cochrane, Ev: *The Many Faces of Venus: The Planet Venus in Ancient Myth and Religion*, Aeon Press, 2001, ISBN 0-9656229-0-9

Dankeskoild, Jim, jdanneskiold@lanl.gov, (505) 667-1640 (04-067):
http://www.lanl.gov/worldview/news/releases/archive/04-067.shtml

David, Leonard: »New Theory: Catastrophe Created Mars' Moons«, Space.com, 7/29/2003

Davidson, H.R. Ellis: *Gods and Myths of Northern Europe*, Penguin Books, 1990, p. 26

Devlet, E.: »Astronomical Objects in Rock Art«, *Astronomical and Astrophysical Transactions*, 1999, Vol. 17, pp. 475-482. From NASA Astrophysics Data System (ADS)

Flannery, K. V., et al: *Science* 158, 445, 1967

Fuhr, Ilse: »On Comets, Comet-like Luminous Apparitions and Meteors«, KRONOS Vol. 7, #4, 1982, ISBN 0361-6584

Kerr, Richard A.: »The Neptune System in Voyager's Afterglow«, *Science*, 245:1450, 1989.

Grant, Michael and Hazel, John: *Who's Who in Classical Mythology*, Oxford University Press, 1973, 1993, p viii

Graves, Robert: *The New Larousse Encyclopedia of Mythology*, Prometheus Press, 1972, p. 258

Groshong, Kimm: »Cassini data reveals new radiation belt around Saturn«, Aug. 6, 2004, http://www.encyclopedia.com/doc/1P2-11023873.html

Hess and Mead: *Introduction to Space Science*, 2nd ed., Gordon and Breach, Inc., p. 823, 1965.

Hogan, James P.: *Kicking the Sacred Cow*, Baen Books, Distributed by Simon & Schuster, 2004, p. 222

Master, S. et al: *Meteoritics and Planetary Science*, 36(9), Suppl., p. A124, 2001; in western Iraq: see *Geographical J.* 123 pp. 231-233; in Argentine: *Nature*, 355, pp. 234-237; in Estonia: see *Meteorics and Planetary Science*, 36 (11) pp. 1507-1514.

Moore, Patrick: *The Planets*, W. W. Norton & Company, 1962, Library of Congress number 62-20547

MSSS (Malin Space Science Systems) and the California Institute of Technology built the MOC using spare hardware from the Mars Observer mission. MSSS operates the camera from its facilities in San Diego, California. http://www.msss.com/mars_images/moc/2003/07/03/

Murrill, Mary Beth, Public Information Office, Jet Propulsion Laboratory, California Institute Of Technology, National Aeronautics And Space Administration: »Nasa's Galileo Finds Giant Iron Core In Jupiter's Moon Io«, May 3, 1996, http://www.jpl.nasa.gov

NASA 2004: http://science.nasa.gov/headlines/y2004/14sep_jupiterdust.htm?list13218

Opik, E. J.: *Science* 153, 255, 1966.

Peratt, A.: »High-Current, Z-Pinch Aurora as Recorded in Antiquity«, *IEEE Transactions on Plasma Science,* December 2004

Peratt, Anthony L.: »Evidence for An Intense Aurora Recorded in Antiquity«, *International Conference on Plasma Science in Jeju, Korea* during June 2-5, 2003, p. 143.

Piccardi, L., and Masse, W. B.: *Myth and Geology,* ISBN: 1-86239-216-1, 13-Digit ISBN: 978-1-86239-216-8, Publisher: GSL, Publication date: 16 February 2007

Ransom, C. J., and Schluter, H.: *Proceedings of the Sixth International Conference on Ionization Phenomena in Gases* (S.E.R.M.A., Paris, 1963), Vol. II, p. 501

Ransom, C. J.: »Bode's Law and the Origin of the Solar System«, *American Journal of Physics,* January 1980, Volume 48, Issue 1, p. 4

Ransom, C. J. & Thornhill, Wal: »Plasma Generated Spherules«, *Bulletin of the American Physical Society*, Vol. 50, #2, April 2005, p. 78

Scott, D.E. and Peratt, A. L.: »The Origin of Petroglyphs – Recordings of a Catastrophic Aurora in Human Prehistory?« *International Conference on Plasma Science, in Jeju, Korea during June 2-5, 2003*, p. 143.

Scott, Donald E.: *The Electric Sky*, Mikamar Publishing, 2006, p. 144

Schatzman, E.: *The Physics of the Solar System*, ed. Rasool, NASA SP 300, p. 409.

Shostak, Seth SETI Institute, 03 February 2005:
http://www.space.com/searchforlife/seti_titan_shostak_050203.html

Sklower, Roberta, S.: Appendix VIII p. 302, in *Mexico Mystique* by F. Waters, 1975.

Velikovsky Affair, p. 117, Stewart quote.

Singer, S. F.: *Science News*, Vol. 109, March 20, 1976, p. 184, notes Icarus (27:197)

Singh, Madanjeet: *The Sun: Symbol of Power and Life*, Harry N. Adams, NY, 1993, p. 62

Smith, F. G.: *Radio Astronomy*, Penguin Books Ltd., 1960

Steele, Duncan: *Marking Time, The Epic Quest to Invent the Perfect Calendar*, John Wiley & Sons, Inc., 2000

Tresidder, Jack: *Dictionary of Symbols*, Chronicle Books, 1997, ISBN 0-8118-1470-X pb.

VanderSluijs, Marinus Anthony: »The World Axis as an Atmospheric Phenomenon«, *Cosmos, The Journal of the Traditional Cosmology Society*, 21. 1 (2005), 3-52

Velikovsky, I.: *Worlds in Collision*, The MacMillan Company, New York, 1950. (MacMillan published *Worlds in Collision* but was forced to drop it soon after publication. Doubleday did not have a textbook division and could not be coerced by people prominent in universities, so Doubleday later published Velikovsky's books.)

Velikovsky, I.: *Earth in Upheaval*, Doubleday, 1955

Veverka, Joseph comments in Cornell release to *Science Daily* in 2000.
http://www.sciencedaily.com/releases/2000/09/000922072457.htm

Wallis, Max: N71-25726 rept. 70-35, Avil. NTIS, Dec. 1970. Later published in *Cosmic Electrodynamics* 3, 45, 1972.

Wescott, Roger Williams: *Predicting the Past, An Exploration of Myth, Science, and Prehistory*, Kronos Press, 2000, ISBN 0-917994-16-7, p. 51

Witzel, Michael, Vala and Iwato: »The Myth of the Hidden Sun in India, Japan, and beyond«, *Electronic Journal of Vedic Studies (EJVS)* 12-1, March 2005, p. 1 (©) ISSN 1084-7561

Index

(**Hint for the user**: Page numbers followed by 'f' or 'ff' refer to the following page(s) as well, usually indicating a more detailed reference to the topic.)

Around the Subject

The Author

Dr. Ruth Velikovsky Sharon learned at the desk of her distinguished father, Dr. Immanuel Velikovsky, a prominent psychiatrist and eminent man of science whose genius engaged even the mind of his friend and contemporary, Albert Einstein.

Dr. Sharon received a B.A and M.A. degrees from New York University and a Ph.D. from the Union Institute and University. She is a graduate of the Center for Modern Psychoanalytic Studies and a certified psychoanalyst.

Books by Ruth Velikovsky Sharon:

- *Aba – The Glory and the Torment* (1995)
- *I Refuse to Raise a Brat* (Co-author with Marilu Henner, 2000)
- *The Truth Behind the Torment* (2003)
- *Shame on You – You Were in My Dream* (2003)
- *The More You Explain ... The Less They Understand* (Co-Author with John C. Seed, M.D. 2005)
- *Imagine Art* (2009)
- *Insights of a Psychoanalyst* (2011)

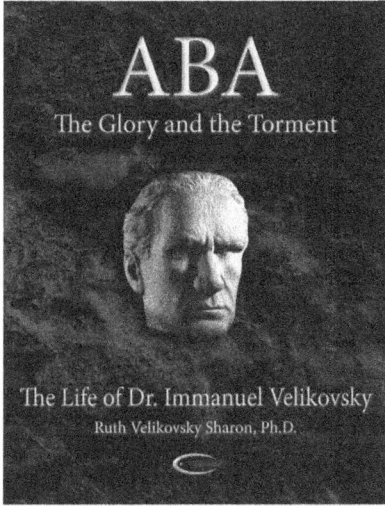

ABA
The Glory and the Torment

The Life of Dr. Immanuel Velikovsky
Ruth Velikovsky Sharon, Ph.D.

ABA – The Glory and the Torment

Ruth Velikovsky Sharon, Ph.D.

Softcover
312 pages
Paradigma Ltd.

ISBN 978-1-906833-20-6

In this book you get to know Immanuel Velikovsky as a person. His daughter Ruth describes his childhood, his family environment and his eventful life.

Using plenty of background information, numerous anecdotes and many photographs she makes us familiar with her father, but also shows the personal dimension of the devastating campaign he encountered in the last decades of his life.

Imagine Art

Works of Art by
Ruth Velikovsky Sharon, Ph.D.
and Elisheva Velikovsky

ISBN 978-1-906833-02-2

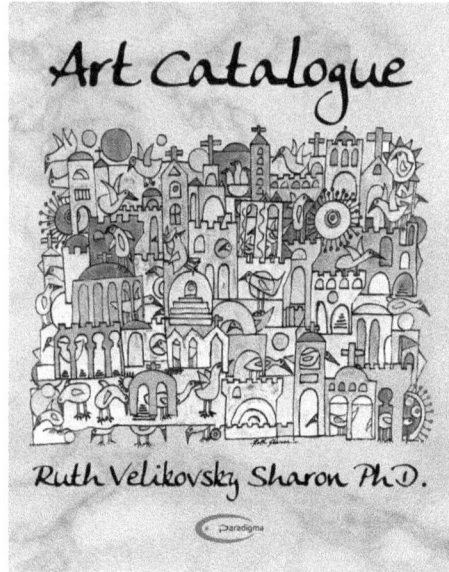

Art Catalogue

Ruth Velikovsky Sharon, Ph.D.

ISBN 978-1-906833-03-9

The name of Velikovsky is mainly known from the scientific and historical discoveries of Immanuel Velikovsky.

Far less known is the artistic dimension in the Velikovsky family, mainly expressed by Elisheva (or "Elis") Velikovsky and Ruth Velikovsky Sharon, PhD., the wife and daughter of Immanuel Velikovsky. For everyone interested in and fond of visual and plastic arts these booklets will give an exhaustive overview of the remarkable range of the works of these two artists.

Shame on You –
You Were in My Dream

Ruth Velikovsky Sharon, Ph.D.

ISBN 978-1-906833-01-5

Finally a new and easy guide to the understanding of dreams, which really makes sense! Ruth Velikovsky Sharon, PhD has developed a completely new understanding of the nature of dreams, which is fascinating because of its simplicity and its practical orientation.

This theory is presented in this book and makes it a valuable guide for parents.

The More You Explain ...
The Less They Understand

Ruth Velikovsky Sharon, Ph.D.
John Cathro Seed, M.D.

ISBN 978-1-906833-00-8

In this, perhaps the most encompassing of her works, Dr. Ruth Velikovsky Sharon brilliantly lifts the veil that shrouds the mystery of psychoanalysis, revealing intrinsic truths that can forever assist us in our journey to self-discovery and growth.

Harvard Medical School Graduate, Dr. John C. Seed's contribution of the Physical Health chapter will enlighten the medical community as well as the average reader, and if abided by, will help prolong life.

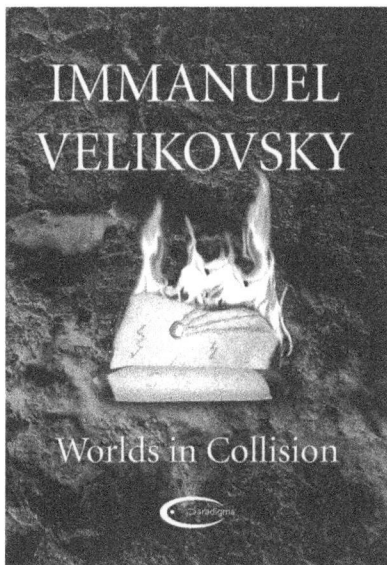

Worlds in Collision

Immanuel Velikovsky

IMMANUEL VELIKOVSKY

Worlds in Collision

436 pages
Paradigma Ltd.

ISBN 978-1-906833-11-4
(Softcover)
978-1-906833-51-0
(Hardcover)

With this book Immanuel Velikovsky first presented the revolutionary results of his 10-year-long interdisciplinary research to the public – and caused an uproar that is still going on today.

Worlds in Collision – written in a brilliant, easily understandable and entertaining style and full to the brim with precise information – can be considered one of the most important and most challenging books in the history of science. Not without reason was this book found open on Einstein's desk after his death.

For all those who have ever wondered about the evolution of the earth, the history of mankind, traditions, religions, mythology or just the world as it is today, *Worlds in Collision* is an absolute MUST-READ!

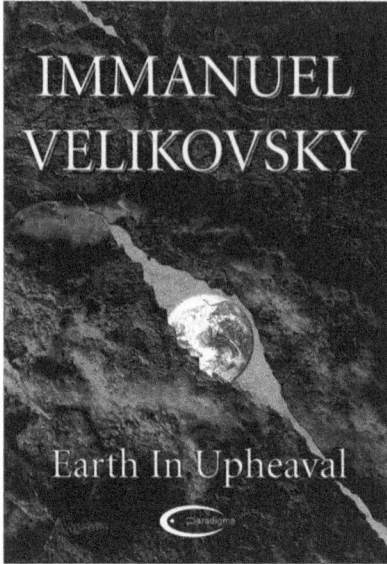

Earth in Upheaval

Immanuel Velikovsky

276 pages
Paradigma Ltd.

ISBN 978-1-906833-12-1
(Softcover)
978-1-906833-52-7
(Hardcover)

After the publication of *Worlds in Collision* Immanuel Velikovsky was confronted with the argument that in the shape of the earth and in the flora and fauna there are no traces of the natural catastrophes he had described.

Therefore a few years later he published *Earth in Upheaval* which not only supports the historical documents by very impressive geological and paleontological material, but even arrives at the same conclusions just based on the testimony of stones and bones.

Earth in Upheaval – a very exactly investigated and easily understandable book – contains material that completely revolutionizes our view of the history of the earth.

For all those who have ever wondered about the evolution of the earth, the formation of mountains and oceans, the origin of coal or fossils, the question of the ice ages and the history of animal and plant species, *Earth in Upheaval* is a MUST-READ!

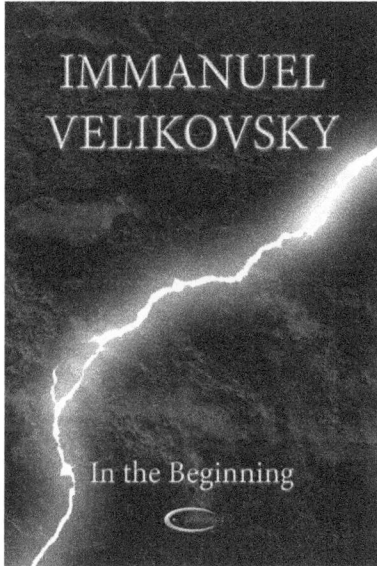

In the Beginning

Immanuel Velikovsky

Paradigma Ltd.

ISBN 978-1-906833-10-7
(Softcover)
978-1-906833-50-3
(Hardcover)

In his main work, the best-selling *Worlds in Collision*, Immanuel Velikovsky gave a detailed reconstruction of two global natural catastrophes based on information handed down by our ancestors.

He mentions there that, as part of his intensive research, he found numerous indications of even more catastrophes that took place earlier in the history of mankind.

In this book, the material collected by Velikovksy about this topic is presented to the public for the first time. His findings show just how turbulent the history of Earth and our planetary system was during the time of mankind and how little we actually know of all that today.

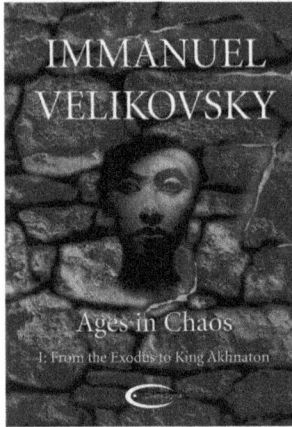

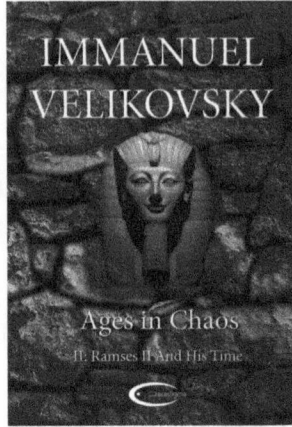

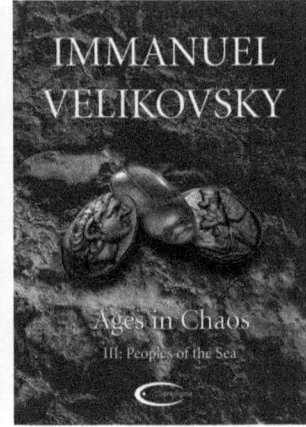

Ages in Chaos

Immanuel Velikovsky

I: From the Exodus to King   II: Ramses II and His Time   III: Peoples of the Sea
    Akhnaton
ISBN 978-1-906833-13-8   ISBN 978-1-906833-14-5   ISBN 978-1-906833-15-2
    978-1-906833-53-4   978-1-906833-54-1   978-1-906833-55-8

In his series *Ages in Chaos*, Immanuel Velikovsky undertakes a reconstruction of the history of antiquity.

With utmost precision and the exciting style of presentation typical for him he shows beyond any doubt what nobody would consider possible: in the conventional history of Egypt – and therefore also of many neighboring cultures – a span of more than 600 years is described which has never happened! This assertion is as unbelievable and outrageous as the assertions in *Worlds in Collision* or *Earth in Upheaval*. But Velikovsky takes us on a detailed and highly interesting journey through the – corrected – history and makes us witness, how many question marks disappear, doubts vanish and corresponding facts from the entire Near East furnish a picture of overall conformity and correctness. In the end you not only wonder how conventional historiography has come into existence, but why it is still taught and published.

Just as Velikovsky became the father of "neo-catastrophism" by *Worlds in Collision*, he became the father of "new chronology" by *Ages in Chaos*.

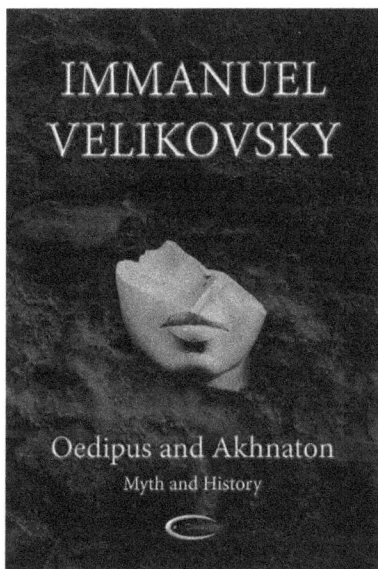

Oedipus and Akhnaton

Immanuel Velikovsky

Paradigma Ltd.

ISBN 978-1-906833-18-3
(Softcover)
978-1-906833-58-9
(Hardcover)

Who hasn't heard of him – Oedipus, the tragic figure from Greek mythology whose shocking fate has moved so many generations, inspired so many writers and even found his way into modern psychology through Sigmund Freud?

Is it conceivable that this figure and his fate was not a creation of human fancy at all but the conversion of real historical happenings?

This question is posed by Immanuel Velikovsky in this book. Like a detective, he takes the reader on a unique investigation full of suspense, breathtaking surprises and insights while meticulously searching for traces of a finding that seems to be even more incredible than the original myth itself.

The most popular pharaonic family of all – Akhnaton along with his wife Nefertiti and his son Tutankhamen – are exposed as the real protagonists of the Oedipus saga.

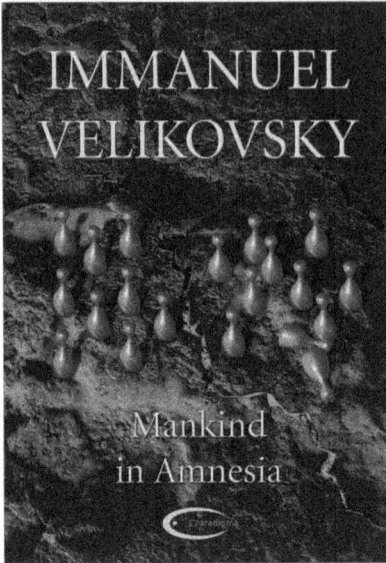

Mankind in Amnesia

Immanuel Velikovsky

196 pages
Paradigma Ltd.

ISBN 978-1-906833-16-9
(Softcover)
978-1-906833-56-5
(Hardcover)

Immanuel Velikovsky called this book the "fulfillment of his oath of Hippocrates – to serve humanity." In this book he returns to his roots as a psychologist and psychoanalytical therapist, yet not with a single person as his patient but with humanity as a whole.

After an extremely revealing overview of the foundations of the various psychoanalytical systems he makes the step into crowd psychology and reopens the case of *Worlds in Collision* from a totally different point of view: as a psychoanalytical case study. This way he shows that the blatant reactions to his theories (which are still going on today) have not been surprising but actually inevitable from a psychological perspective – which equally holds for those who have defined our view of the world. At the same time he is able to reclassify the theories of Siegmund Freud and of C. G. Jung by finding a common basis for them.

A journey through history, religion, mythology and art shows the overall range of the collective trauma and gives us – the patients – a message of extraordinary urgency and importance for the future.

www.ingramcontent.com/pod-product-compliance
Lightning Source LLC
Chambersburg PA
CBHW021228090426
42740CB00006B/438